THE CHALLENGE OF ORIENTEERING

The Challenge of
ORIENTEERING

Gordon Pirie

LINE ILLUSTRATIONS BY E. BROOKS

PELHAM BOOKS

First published in Great Britain by
PELHAM BOOKS LTD
26 *Bloomsbury Street*
London, W.C.1
1968
© 1968 *by Gordon Pirie*

7207 0167 8

Set and printed in Great Britain by
Tonbridge Printers Ltd, Peach Hall Works, Tonbridge, Kent,
in Times ten on twelve point, and bound by
James Burn at Esher, Surrey

CONTENTS

ILLUSTRATIONS

ACKNOWLEDGEMENTS

The author records his grateful thanks to the many Swedish friends who so generously supplied him with photographs for use in this book. Thanks are also due to the following for permission to reproduce photographs in which they hold copyright: Christian Bonington and *Weekend Telegraph*, 1; Hands Sundberg, 5; Hilding Mickelsson, 7; Harold Persson, 8; Pressens Bild AB, 10, 34; HT-Bild, 11, 33; B. J. Ward Ltd., 17–21; Stenbergs Bilder, 14; B. M. Bild AB, 22; P. O. Ek, 23; Magnus Johnson, 24; Ulf Bergman, 25; Aftonbladet, 26; Hons Persson, 27; Robert Lundqvist, 28; James Engman, 29; Nerikes Allehanda, 30; Lars K. Larsson, 32

In illustration 12, extracts 18, 19, 22, 23, 28, 35, 36, 37, 39, 40, 41, 42, 43, 44, 45, 46, 50, 51 are reproduced from Ordnance Survey maps with the sanction of the Controller of H.M. Stationery Office. Crown Copyright reserved.

Foreword

by Baron Gösta 'Rak' Lagerfelt

of Stockholms Orienteringsklubb, Sweden
One of the best known pioneers of international Orienteering

The sport of orienteering has all the significance of an adventure. Every new competition has the charm of discovery, a new exciting thrill, the attraction of uncertainty.

It is a sport of endless variation and richness. And yet it is a sport which is precise: a hard sport which requires much from its participants who have reached top class; a sport with championships of its own, associations of its own, and special clubs of its own. It is also a sport which is highly progressive, not only in England, but viewed internationally.

Yes, orienteering is definitely on the move at the present time. In a way it fills a vacuum in the diverse range of sports which our civilisation has developed over many decades, for it supplies a real need in the age of development in which modern sport now finds itself. Orienteering is completely free from the problems of 'professionalism', free both from the struggle for records and from the pursuit of unattainable standards.

Orienteering is not 'hedged in' by sports-fields and spectators – it is practised in the loveliest, most beautiful and most varied of all sporting venues: in the heart of nature, in forests and in woods, with their stimulating atmosphere and perpetually changing scenes.

You should experience the atmosphere of a big orienteering competition in Sweden, the country where the sport originated. It is like a kind of festival. The competing runners assemble at the meeting point, and since nobody arrives alone, they have usually brought the whole family to share in the fun. Junior leaders of the clubs also have their cars filled with alert youngsters. It is a point of honour to

9

try to find beautiful spots for the 'finish' of the big orienteering runs. Everybody develops a strong feeling for the beauties of unspoiled nature, realising that they are precious gifts which cannot be valued too highly in our present hectic age. The sport of orienteering creates this feeling and so gives added value to our existence.

A big orienteering competition consists of a great number of classes. In the same orienteering competition but on different courses, of varied degrees of difficulty and toughness, there are top-class runners who are as well trained as the top men in athletics, twelve-year-old boys and girls, and grey-haired older men approaching their sixties, who find the sport a stimulating way of staying young in mind and body. Each competitor goes in for the particular event best suited to his age and qualifications, but all categories thoroughly enjoy their adventures in the forest – everybody has a really good time.

It is not difficult to imagine what a wonderful time a youngster has, taking part in the same competition as his father and also, perhaps, his mother. Those who are too young to enter wait, in great excitement, at the 'finish', and applaud wildly when dad or mum shows up in a more or less expert-style finish! Many fields of sport create problems for family life. Orienteering has shown itself able to unite the family together in a lovely, refreshing Sunday sport which suits everybody.

An advanced course for top-class competitors in a big competition is not easy to cover in a time which gives chance of victory. Competition is awfully keen in the great international events, and the technique and experience of the runners are enormous. To win a race in a qualified competition in Scandinavia requires much experience, gathered during many orienteering runs, and much training to improve actual running ability. However, success does not by any means depend solely on how well trained one is in running. You do not win in orienteering just by running. You have to use your head too. Judgment and ability are tested over and over again during an orienteering run. The capacity to concentrate; the ability to be calm at the right moment; to ascertain one's position quickly and with a clear head when some error, large or small, has been made and then has to be corrected without delay; to decide exactly where on the map one is. All these advanced brain gymnastics have to be performed under strong physical tension.

All orienteering runners were, of course, once beginners and know that there are innumerable ways of making mistakes. To learn from the mistakes one has made is itself an education. Orienteering is an education. Some who have newly become orienteering enthusiasts, lose their enthusiasm when they have been lost a couple of times and have had to appear at the 'finish' without having found all the control points. They will never experience the sheer fun of the sport unless they keep trying. Others who have a little more will-power, who are, perhaps, a little stubborn and who are eager for victory, overcome this difficult obstacle which every competitor has to face. Suddenly they find that everything works, suddenly they find that they know how to do it. They then become aware of all the attractions the sport has to offer.

During an orienteering run you have to discipline yourself. And you have to keep your head clear and your judgment functioning, especially on the last few kilometres of a long, hard course. In orienteering, tiredness of the brain is much more disastrous than tiredness of the legs. Certainly, you lose time by running slowly, but you lose a lot more by running in the wrong direction!

Enthusiasts have called orienteering the best sport in the world. Different sports, however, are difficult to compare, and there are certainly many sports with considerable appeal. However, orienteering is, without doubt, one of the most attractive. You who read this and who would like to try it, must realise that orienteering is hard to describe and demonstrate. You really have to try it for yourself to be able to judge what it is really like. No spectator at the 'finish' of an orienteering run can really appreciate all the varied experiences which one single run produces for each of the competitors. Even if you could follow a runner around the course in a helicopter, you would not be able to share in all the drama and fascination which an orienteering run offers.

You can get some idea of what it all means if you are stationed as an official at one of the control points on the course; as you stand by the red flag of the control you will see the runners appearing through the forest. One will come, at high speed, directly to the control from the correct direction, absolutely sure of himself. At the control, he will work methodically with his map and compass as he decides how he is to tackle the problems of the next part of the course. Another runner will appear from the wrong direction, considerably

11

delayed and anxious to make up for the minutes he has lost, perhaps too anxious! Later, maybe you will catch a glimpse of a third man some 50 metres away in the forest, and just about to miss the control – either because he is not observant enough or because he does not know that right now is the time to look and look and look again, since the flag just has to be close by. How soon before he has the situation sorted out? It is exactly in tense moments like these during the competition that the runners' final positions will be decided. And it is here that experience or calm nerves will most often make all the difference. When will you again see the runner whom you observed among the trees? Will it take half a minute before he gets back on the right track, or has he lost his bearings so much that it will take him several minutes before he has found the right way?

The sign of the skilled expert orienteerer is often his ability to correct quickly the small mistakes without which it is seldom possible to cover a long orienteering course. The difficult thing is to know where one is at any given moment, and not to lose contact with the map at any stage of the course. By counting one's steps, one should always know exactly how far one has run in the forest towards the difficult control from the nearest certain point of location. An expert runner who has made up his mind to win must practise a tactic which is basically a continual weighing up of speed against certainty. You do not achieve great victories in orienteering without taking chances to a certain degree. Of course, if the taking of chances is carried too far, it will often result in serious error and a loss of time. But remember, if the runner is too careful, the speed will not be enough.

In events run on athletics tracks, it is sometimes possible, and not too difficult, to guess who the winner, or at least the first three, will be. In orienteering nothing is certain. The man who won the last run by a good and safe margin may fall into a small error on his next outing and have to be satisfied with a much less honourable position in the results list. That demonstrates another of the educational aspects of orienteering. It teaches you to be humble, to take success with calmness and with gratitude. You never find anyone with the attitude of 'I'm the greatest' in orienteering. There is always a great understanding and willingness to help on the part of the experienced, towards the novices, who, of course, make real 'beginner's' mistakes. There is an especially fine spirit of companionship and loyalty among these 'sportsmen of the woods'.

It cannot be said that orienteering is a sport which is particularly easy to arrange. Above all, the setting of the course requires good judgment and great experience. Thick books have been written on the difficult art of setting courses, and many ideas and fashions have influenced the technique of course-setting during the years when the most satisfactory methods of ensuring courses of generally high standards were being evolved.

Generally speaking, the more the arts and skills of orienteering are tested, the better the course. The more varied the problems the runner is confronted with, and has to overcome, the better. The more complicated the different decisions he has to make during the run, the more interesting the choice of routes he is offered between controls, the more satisfying will the course prove. It should be planned so that skill and not chance decides the competition, allied with good training and sound judgment on the part of the runner.

As interesting and inspiring as the running is in its way, as fascinating as is the task of setting a really good course, it is not a job that can be done half-heartedly. It takes time and calls for repeated and careful thought, and for imagination. Just the matter of a millimetre one way or the other on the map in the siting of a control, may make the route between two controls decidedly better, disguise a given choice of route, or open up a number of alternatives for the runner to choose from. A course-maker who has never been an orienteering runner himself can hardly prepare a really good course. That does not necessarily mean that every good runner can become as good a course-maker! One thing is sure, however: The 'wanderings about' that a course-maker makes when he examines his course in the planned area have much the same thrill of discovery as any expedition to some far country. It is the most rewarding job for an official in the world of sport.

The sport of orienteering was born in Sweden. It is especially suited to the types of forest and wild country which you find there. In spite of primitive maps, it developed tremendously during the twenties, thirties and forties. At the end of the fifties, revolutionary events took place in Scandinavian orienteering. The maps were considerably improved – this by the orienteering people themselves.

13

They drew their own maps, and of course made sure that these contained all the special requirements an orienteerer would need on his map. In the sixties the map scale became 1:25,000, after previously having mostly been 1:50,000, and earlier even 1:100,000. This increased the precision and decreased the 'chancy' elements in the sport. But the wonderful charm remained. Many people now seriously began to realise that here were opportunities for a new world-wide sport.

It was at this time that Swedish pioneers began to take an interest in spreading orienteering outside Scandinavia. Elsewhere in Europe there was excellent material for maps, and the feeling for good sport in combination with a fresh outdoor life was in the blood of many nations. The problem was only to create the spark which would start the flame: to find the right leaders with an enthusiasm not easily dismayed, and the real pioneering spirit.

I had the opportunity, which I prize very highly, of introducing orienteering to many countries where the sport is now established. As late as 1958, when the sport was first introduced to West Germany, many people still thought that orienteering as an international sport was something quite impossible, and that its introduction into Germany was to be considered more of a novelty than as a practical possibility for general participation. This way of thinking has proved to be completely wrong, and development outside Scandinavia has been very favourable. The first European championships were held as early as 1962, and the first World championships in 1966.

Among the countries where the seeds of orienteering soon found fertile soil in which to grow, and where development was rapid, was Great Britain. Personally I was not at all surprised at this. We sports-minded Swedes well know that few people have a better developed sporting sense than the British. When I was working on the introduction of the sport into Great Britain, many 'wise' advisers told me that such a generally conservative people would not accept a new sport, because they regarded themselves as having already invented all the sports which were worth inventing! And, besides, my advisers said, there is no suitable terrain for orienteering either in England or in Scotland!

Both opinions were completely wrong. The British have proved that they *are* broad-minded in sporting matters, and that they are willing to accept a new sport quickly and effectively when it is a good sport. There is also a tremendous amount of very good terrain for orienteering in Britain, even on the outskirts of the big cities – even if the countryside differs in many aspects from that of Scandinavia.

Introductory events, run on Swedish lines, were held in Sherwood Forest, outside Nottingham, in 1959, and near the little Scottish town of Dunkeld, Perthshire, in 1962. Even so, orienteering did not really receive the 'go-ahead' in Britain until athletes with world reputations – Pirie, Brasher, Disley, Tulloh and others – began to take an interest in the infant sport.

Orienteering then rapidly made a break-though. An English Orienteering Association was founded which later, in accordance with the wishes of the International Association of Orienteering, was to become the British Orienteering Federation. The Federation is administered by hard-working and devoted people, people with a genuine sense of the sport's special character. There is every reason to predict a bright future for British orienteering. Certainly, no-one wishes the sport in Britain a brighter future more sincerely than the author of this Foreword.

It is significant that enthusiasm for orienteering, the sport of forest and open country, is most easily aroused in the cities, simply because it is pure 'medicine for the soul' for overworked city dwellers in London as well as in Dortmund, Zurich as in Stockholm, Prague as in Manchester. The Olympic gold medallist Chris Brasher, who is both a skilled journalist and an orienteer, has said in a refreshing article that an orienteering run is about the most 100 per cent. relaxing activity you can experience. During such a run, you are so exclusively concerned with the fascinating and varied problems which continually arise, that you completely forget all the problems or difficulties connected with home or work. It provides a cleansing of the brain and the soul which is superior to most cures and medicines. Life, in fact, at its best.

This has long been appreciated in Sweden. There, orienteering actually has a place, if not on the weekly timetable in the schools, at least in the teaching curriculum. Every Swedish pupil is given instruction in orienteering. If they develop an understanding and feeling for it, then they will have a lifetime hobby. Thousands have already discovered this.

This book is written by a first-class instructor on the sport. In a

15

very short time, Gordon Pirie has, with great determination, talent and wise application, trained himself up to world-class as an orienteering runner. No Englishman can discuss the sport with greater knowledge of its international aspects, or with a wider experience of its background to back up his judgments and his excellent advice. Few have worked harder to make orienteering international than the author of this foreword, and I want to emphasise the enormous significance Gordon Pirie's connection with orienteering has had in relation to the rapid development of the sport, not only in Great Britain but also on the international scene.

Now read his book. Read and learn. Become enthusiastic. And may I welcome you to the forests, woods, and into the country. Welcome you to your first orienteering run, a really exciting and entertaining experience.

What wonderful times you have ahead of you as orienteerers! The excitement of competition, the thrill of the 'uncertain', the great adventure of the forests: these are the bait we are offering you. You just have to open your mouths and bite. Then you are hooked. Congratulations!

Baron Gösta 'Rak' Lagerfelt,
Stockholms Orienteringsklubb,
Sweden.

CHAPTER ONE

What is Orienteering?

'To a man of imagination a map is a window to adventure'
Sir Francis Chichester

The Swede, Major Killander, devised a brilliant new sport in 1919 which called for the use of skills not needed nor developed by any other single sport. The participant had to find his way across country in the virgin forest of Sweden. The idea was to reach specific points on the map and return to the start as quickly as possible.

Thus was born the modern sport of Orienteering. The first 'Orienteerers' had very sketchy maps showing lakes, marshes, log cabins and the shape of forests and their interlacing paths, tracks and streams. A primitive compass was also carried.

The sport of Orienteering soon exploded in popularity and today there are hundreds of thousands of Orienteering enthusiasts in Scandinavia alone. The present second-stage acceleration of interest embraces all Central European countries and Great Britain. From 1964 the sport of Orienteering has been put on a sound footing by the enthusiasm of an older generation of semi-retired athletes and the advent of a school-age group of enthusiasts. Since athletics has developed into a serious, demanding business, fit only for those with extraordinary qualities in a physical and psychological sense, the masses have become divorced from athletics for pleasure and the satisfaction of achievement is no longer within their reach.

Orienteering offers to all a unique mixture of mental exercise and the advantages to be derived from physical effort. Because of the need to be as 'wily as a fox' to find one's way in Orienteering, the successful completion of the Orienteering course is satisfying in much the same way as is finishing a crossword or any other game of wits. The bonus of physical well-being derived whilst you solve the knotty problems of Orienteering makes this sport the best gift that has been devised for civilisation's sagging health standards. In Orienteering the exercise element is comfortably sandwiched in a series of intriguing situations needing thought, attention and concentration. Many is the Orienteering event which has provided me with moments of satisfying pleasure – yet also hours of oblivion from the cares of life – and provided the physical stimulus necessary to keep the body in energetic and vigorous condition. Remarkably, this achievement of 'sound mind and body' through Orienteering comes without any regimentation, sacrifice or suffering which accompany the organised and often soul-killing traditional sports.

Yes, Orienteering is a fascinating sport in which the 'sport' attempts to orientate himself in strange countryside with the aid of a map and compass and then find his way as quickly as he can to specific points indicated on his map. Orienteering, therefore, develops skill in map-reading and in reconciling the map's 'picture' to the features of the terrain to which it relates. The orienteerer has to choose the best route for himself between the specific points he must visit, and this is the intriguing part of the sport. Is the path on my map still there on the ground? Will it be quicker to take a long, easy route rather than the direct and difficult one involving crossing a hill or valley through thick woods?

There are many different routes to be taken in well-organised Orienteering races – but no one direct and simple path which everyone may automatically follow. The specific point which the orienteerer seeks is called a 'control point' and a red flag shows him his target when he has reached its close proximity. Control points may be at the site of an old well, a spring, a small bridge over a stream or in a thickly wooded gulley. The orienteerer is furnished with a clue description that tells him the location and what to look for at each control point. The clever orienteerer can imagine the picture his map projects and so knows immediately he reaches the control point – even before seeing the flag – that he is in the right spot.

The challenge of the unknown and the achievement of reaching a control point is extremely satisfying to intellect and physique alike. Orienteering is a gift to the masses who can derive pure satisfaction, enjoyment and good health while remaining undedicated and quite normal people.

As a champion athlete I wrongly assumed that I might step into immediate success in Orienteering, but I was in for a rude shock. My Orienteering career started in 1964 when, thanks to England's pioneer, John Disley, the Olympic steeplechaser, I was attracted to the sport. One Sunday morning I gathered my athletic kit and answered the call to battle at Peaslake School in the heart of Surrey. John gave me a compass and a little advice. Of course, I thought I knew all the answers! I paid my entry fee of half a crown and received a map and a slip of paper with squares on it. The squares were to accommodate the expected stamp marks from markers which were hung on each control point. This was to prove my visits to them! Lastly I was given a list of mysterious clues for the control points: No. 1 'At the path junction', No. 2 'Between the hills' – I cannot remember the other half-dozen for reasons you will understand from my story!

Before starting, there was no 'moment of truth' – no tension among the orienteerers such as I had experienced in years of top-class athletics. Everyone chatted amiably and the almost casual atmosphere was wonderfully refreshing. One lad was clad in climbing boots and plus-fours. He held a two-foot square board with his map clipped neatly on it. I could not resist pointing out that he could not hope to cover the ground very quickly in all that gear. This lad was Graham Westbrook, who had won the previous event – dressed like that! I was silenced but thought, 'I'll run that fellow into the ground!'

The crowd slowly thinned as, one by one, they were dispatched into the surrounding woods at one-minute intervals. Soon it was my turn. 'Another minute and you're off!' said the starter. My pulse raced and I looked at the control points I had carefully copied from the master map and joined up into a neat, numbered circuit of circles and lines with my red ballpoint. 'Thirty seconds to go!' shouted the time-keeper. I gripped my compass in my right hand – knuckles showing white with the tension .'Ten seconds to go!' he whispered. Feet pawing at the tarmac of the playground, I crouched and propelled myself away at breakneck speed on 'Zero!' Down the path, turn left, straight on down the hill. Stop, look at map – not too certainly – glance foolishly at compass. I reached No. 1 quite easily, stamped my control card and set off confidently for No. 2.

'This is easy', thought the 'new champion'. I followed my compass-bearing from the map, head down, bulldozing my way through thick brush, pine trees, brambles and bracken and on to a broad path cutting diagonally across my route. There was Westbrook! He was walking along the path surveying his map as if he were reading the Sunday papers. I was elated because he had started long before me. I raced by, redoubling my efforts in my jubilation, and disappeared into the wilderness once more.

Some time later I had to admit that all my charging about had been in vain. I was lost. Other wanderers tagged on to me as I rushed here and there, scouring the forest. Eventually, by process of elimination and more by accident than judgment, I found No. 2, and continued haphazardly across country like the Pied Piper with a tail of faithful followers - all lost but enjoying ourselves!

After about one and a half hours I met a lady in a lane and, thanks to her assistance, found our location. This advice-seeking is forbidden in Orienteering – so don't do it unless you are in the position I was in at Peaslake. It turned out to my surprise we were within a few hundred yards of the school where we had started. By this time I was quite tired, so returned to the school to discover that Graham Westbrook had already won and gone home!

There are several lessons to be learnt from my Peaslake experience. Never send a novice orienteerer off to complete a whole course. Either send an experienced orienteerer with him so that the novice may learn as he goes along, or only give the novice the simple task of visiting two or three controls close to the start. Had I not been so determined, that first experience of Orienteering would have destroyed all my interest and I should have been lost to the sport.

As for the others who followed me at Peaslake, this is another lesson. Never take any notice of the other competitor – concentrate on your map, compass and the terrain. If you follow someone else you are defeating yourself in the long run, for in Orienteering you must learn to do the job alone. Many is the time I have been quite alone in some strange neck of the woods and my own judgment and skill in Orienteering have enabled me to find my way. Regard the others as incorrect. But note their activities, for often you yourself can be wrong!

What do you do in the chance encounter with a competitor travelling at speed in the opposite direction? Is he right? Am I

20

right? Has he just found what I am looking for? Or has an irate land-owner just given him the benefit of his buckshot? More than likely one of you is lost, or you may both be searching for completely different controls. Seeking or giving advice is frowned upon – it is best to remain silent and give only polite hand signals. Crafty comments are not ruled out. 'Have you seen No. 3?' you query – as you race on to No. 4!

Behaviour at the control points is important. Too many in-experienced orienteerers stand by the control point for minutes studying their maps. Worse still, they wear brightly-coloured clothing and stand out like a beacon to the incoming runners. In Scandinavia the standard drab camouflage colours of black, brown, dark green and grey are worn. Orienteerers shouldn't give away the control points. If others are around crawl the last yards to and from the control points.

When leaving a control never do so in such a way as to help others. Run slowly until out of sight, changing direction a little and even hesitating and reading the map. Glance round as if you are still searching the vicinity. When you are well clear you then race off in a bee-line for the next control. If I am being followed by a fellow orienteerer, I race hard to drop him or nip off into a thicket or make a diversion. Once you lose a man who is using you as a pioneer, he is in real trouble because he will have lost his position on the map as he struggled to keep contact with you!

The most dangerous situation in Orienteering is when you have lost your own position on the map. As I run along I reconcile every feature on the map with the ground like stepping-stones across a lake. When lost, the orienteerer must stop and think, resisting the panic-driven reaction of racing onwards in the hope of running across some clue to his whereabouts. Expert orienteerers, when lost, quickly find themselves by logic. In fact it is a saying that the orienteerer when lost knows where he is lost.

The self-control and development of logical judgment is valuable training and transferable to all aspects of life. Orienteering develops self-confidence, patience, self-reliance, physical fitness and a realisation that a person is not an infallible machine. The individual aspect of the sport is unique. You are alone, depending upon your own decisions and needing the courage of your convictions in situations of stress and excitement when, perhaps, the mind is dulled by fatigue. All this means that Orienteering has tremendous value in an educational sense. It offers a most fascinating and stimulating challenge that cannot be matched by any other single sport or single educational activity.

Orienteering is a mixture of geography, map-reading, mathematics, intellect and character-training as well as physical education. Orienteering is enjoyable, amusing, time-consuming and absolutely harmless. The sport extends beyond the competitive time; the examination of routes and courses and the comparison of techniques offer endless hours of interesting discussion.

The true experience of Orienteering is in participation, and the hours of enjoyment are recorded on your well-handled map and indelibly imprinted in your memory. The possibilities of what you might have done with the application of more skill remain a mystery held captive by the meticulously red-inked circles and lines of your Orienteering course.

It is true to say that my few years of Orienteering have provided a greater return than two decades in the regimentation and strait jacket of athletics.

Orienteering shows up the fallibility of the human brain in situations of stress and exhaustion.

A Finnish Gold Medallist course setter, who shall be anonymous, told me his story over a coffee at Solvalla Sports Institute in October, 1966, whilst I was in Finland for the Inaugural World Championships. It was snowing outside. The pine and silver birch trees showed starkly against the lake below. My Finnish friend told many stories as we pored over hundreds of maps that his years in Orienteering had gathered up into a compact file of meticulous method which culminated in his achieving the coveted Gold Medal award. Only those with the greatest skill and knowledge of Orienteering can be in this elite position.

Among his many tales of races laced with the excitement of winning and the frustrations of missing a control, the story which amused him and me most was one concerned with a simple mistake he made only the same year. On leaving a control he had taken a bearing and set off, confidently following his compass needle. This was an automatic motion for him – he had done it many thousands of times before. He jumped from rock to rock, ran through a small moss (marshy land), then between the pine trees – and suddenly stopped in his tracks. It was wrong – the forest didn't agree with the map! There wasn't a moss on his correct route, and it dawned on him, unbelievably, that he was running the opposite way to his correct direction of travel. Quickly, consulting his map, he checked his course bearing. He was exactly 180° wrong. He had run about two hundred metres in the wrong direction!

Of course experience can lull the wits of the cleverest person. How about the orienteerer who had to cross a railway? He stood on the iron bridge wrestling hopelessly with his compass for a good five minutes before giving up in disgust. Or the English International cross country runner who ran out of the school buildings where the Orienteering race started – and stood next to a parked car? He had difficulty in making a 'fix' with his compass that tallied with his logical dead reckoning! – So don't forget to discard all metal objects!

In Orienteering we always seek the easiest route or the less physically demanding way of crossing the terrain. You don't cross a swamp if you can circumnavigate it by a nice path. A true story of a night event is from an orienteerer who saw to his horror, in the light of his head torch, that his course couldn't avoid a broad and what turned out to be a chest-deep and ice-cold stream. Half way across he was scared out of his wits by a louder and louder thumping over-head. He swung his torch upwards and saw a fellow competitor running across a superb footbridge built for drier pedestrianism!

A dirty trick to play – Heaven forbid! – is to reverse the compass of a competitor. This is a joke carried out in 'practical joke' Orienteer-ing at festival times in Sweden. The equipment needed is a piece of metal that fits in the palm of the hand and is very strongly magnet-ised. It is held for a moment over the Orienteering compass and reverses the polarity of the compass needle. Hard luck on the owner of the compass!

The compass, therefore, needs looking after carefully. It is a very personal instrument and should be kept close to the heart. For safety the compass has a cord which you attach round the wrist. This is a nuisance and to start with one might discard it as worthless. How-ever, after running at speed through bushes and having the compass whipped out of one's hand by a tree branch, then searching on hands and knees over several square yards of bramble or bracken, one reverts to the safety cord. The only drawback I have found is that some safety cords are too strong, and this comes to light when you need to jump off rocks or run down steep wooded slopes. It is quite disconcerting to be stopped suddenly, garrotted round the wrist by the safety cord as the compass is snatched by a strong tree fork – you can't win!

In Scandinavia, Orienteering is a test of ability to find control points in unknown and wild territory. It is also an opportunity for organisers to create an aura of mystery and the setting for a trial of the mental strength of the orienteerer, even before he is in possession of his map and on the course. Misleading instructions are usually put out; while the competitors assemble the officials carry on guarded whisperings away from us. We don't know where the event is to start. There are miles and miles of forest lying in every direction, all of it capable of swallowing a whole army without trace in its mossy forests and rocky undulations. Next time I even expect blinds to be drawn over the bus windows as we are transported through the forest.

The competitors are disgorged from the buses at a very early hour in the morning, usually about 8.30 if we are due to start racing at 10.30. Why? Because you then set off one hour before your start time for a heavily-wooded spot, usually mosquito-inhabited, where your senses are completely disorientated. From here you proceed down a mysterious trail of streamers in the bushes to a pre-start for documentation. By this time all your friends have gone ahead or been left behind. The few competitors in your time limbo are fearsome Vikings – magnificent men who can run Orienteering in their sleep and are as strong as lions. You haven't a chance against them. Incidentally, they are also the fellows you race by in the forest. Eventually the map is pressed into your shaking hands in some leafy grove, also mosquito-infested. The last official control before you dive alone into the green engulfing wilderness is usually manned by beautiful blondes who smile coyly as they wish you 'Morn, Morn'. A Swedish good morning!

Many is the time I have been completely played out by nervous exhaustion before starting the competition. The funny thing is that the competent orienteerer still sets off like a rocket into the newest wilderness despite all the efforts of the organiser to fool him. It is the novice who suffers nervous prostration or breaks down.

Most races in England have yet to attain this exhausting level for me and we enjoy ourselves in a more relaxed atmosphere – things

24

The author: first English Orienteering Champion, 1966; first British Orienteering Champion, 1967, and Champion again in 1968

'At the top of the cliff'. Controls should be chosen carefully, with clear and concise definitions

(*Left*) In spite of tension, be accurate and quick. Here a competitor copies the course on to his map from a master map. (*Below*) Just before the start. Excitement mounts as competitors receive their maps

A Swedish *Tiomila* (massed) start. The world's elite orienteerers start on their rapid way – ten-man teams, covering ten stages, over ten Swedish miles. The finish is a day away

(*Above left*) The Orienteerer savours all the beauty and solitude of the wilds.
(*Above right*) A Champion's finish. Bertil Norman, a Swedish orienteering champion, throws the last ounce of energy into a dramatic sprint finish.
(*Below left*) Always take the easiest route. (*Below right*) A fast track saves time and energy

are quite casual at times. The writing is on the wall, though, for an English Area Championship bears the savage threat: 'Anyone not back before 4 p.m. will be barred from future events'. As the start is at 10 a.m., anyone not back before 4 p.m. is lying in the woods or has given up in disgust – never to try Orienteering again, anyway.

Lastly, a word of advice. Don't wear a metal watch strap or any magnetic watch, or metal buttons or metal map-holder – or have metal fillings in your teeth. Remember that finest and most beloved Orienteering friend – your compass!

PRACTICAL USES FOR ORIENTEERING

The skills of Orienteering are applicable to a wide range of activities. The outdoor hobbies of hiking, mountaineering, scouting and all trips on foot can be made more interesting and rewarding by a good level of Orienteering skills. For the more serious necessities of military activities, surveying or engineering and exploring in unknown territory, Orienteering ability is an indispensable asset.

For all who wish to develop physical fitness without its being a bore, then Orienteering is the finest activity. Any athlete will become fitter through Orienteering, and he will benefit enormously from casting away the regimes of the athletic world.

The very fact that all ages participate in Orienteering means that it is a sport for all – no barriers exist whatever your physical condition or age. Events provide a full range of courses: 'Wayfarers' are those who like a hike; 'Elite Orienteerers' are the minority who do Orienteering as an exciting, demanding competition. Courses vary from a mile to ten miles and you are free to go as you wish – no sport could be freer for the competitor - and when you have tasted the curiously interesting flavour of Orienteering you will always come back for more.

CHAPTER TWO

Types of Races

Orienteering is unique in practice because a single course can be arranged in so many permutations and combinations giving varying degrees of difficulty. In its most casual aspect you may wander through beautiful scenery with a map and compass, navigating from feature to feature, savouring the views and fresh air at your leisure. This we call Wayfaring, and in every Orienteering event there is a course devised for the benefit of the young and old and any hiker who wishes to treat the sport of Orienteering as an easy and interesting healthy relaxation.

At the other end of the scale, those who wish to taste the excitement and the exertions of cut-throat competitive Orienteering can take part at the elite and championship level. Because of the rare qualities that Orienteering possesses we can cater for every physical, and psychological type and desire in one competition.

Most events have to be organised with meticulous care involving weeks of hard work and some loss of sleep. In the championship and international events, and well-organised and well-supported club events that we enjoy, there is a small group of enthusiastic orienteerers who have put in many hours to organise their event. The chance to organise Orienteering races is not to be missed, since in doing this one may learn more about the skills of map-reading, locating points on the ground, pacing distance and direction-finding than one can gather in competing in half a dozen races.

I would, however, tend to disagree with leading authorities who claim that one is pitting one's wits against the competitor's in organising races. This is because of the fact that a course setter has days to study the map and relate it to the ground at his leisure and, thus, becomes very familiar with every hollow and bush. This destroys completely the aura of mystery and excitement existing in all Orienteering races when time is short and the countryside is quite foreign to the competitor. Even the second visit to one area of previously unknown terrain renders it 'harmless' from the point of view of Orienteering. Therefore the organiser cannot savour the true excitement of the event. It is possible nearly to halve your circuit time on the second occasion that you run round an Orienteering course. Rather is the organiser the servant of the competitors, and we have to acknowledge that the sport exists thanks to the organisers.

The many mutations of the Orienteering event are like a menu you select from and then savour as you wish. Even during the event you have free choice of your route (excepting line events which I describe later – but these are more a form of training venture and soon lose their attraction for a skilled orienteerer). There are footpaths you may stroll or race down or, if you are impatient, the penetration of any kind of difficulty beckons to you. One can travel as straight as an arrow over hill and dale, through swamp and forest – but avoiding private areas – in a beeline towards the next control point. This 'penetration' method needs skill in maintaining direction and great strength and determination to negotiate what can be exhausting territory. You also need keen eyesight – one eye on the route ahead, another on the compass – and yet still alert for the pitfalls underfoot and tree branches at eye level. Many is the time I have tumbled over obstacles or sprung off wire fences hidden in the forest while bull-dozing across country. The decision rests with you – your desires and common sense will decide – for if there is a swift route by a path, track or road involving a minor deviation, this will be taken and you always arrive before the 'bulldozer in the bush'. Naturally many courses offer a bonus to 'bulldozers' when they are strong and fit.

The perambulation from control to control, no matter what its type and direction, is always rewarded by the sight of that welcoming red control flag. Stamping your check card to prove your success is a terrific morale-booster. The wilting mind and body are resuscitated magically by this red flag 'tonic'. You did it all alone and despite

27

those nagging doubts in your mind as to your ability. You made it! This is how the orienteerer measures success, together with the fact that he is never lost completely. Apparently lost, perhaps, yet knowing in a moment that he is standing 'there' on the map after a quick assessment of the terrain.

The results sheet printed after the event is only the skeleton of the race. The real flesh and blood of the sport is to be savoured by participation – getting lost, finding yourself, then finding the controls – and on doing this, uttering Sir Francis Chichester's famous navigator's cry 'Spot On'! No one else knows how big a liar you are!

Orienteering success springs from mistakes which you emblazon upon your mind. After races many is the cry, 'What a stupid thing I did there!', when competitors go over their route on the bedraggled maps which they clung to over hill and dale as their only 'lifeline' with the outside world – their key to finishing!

One important rule in all races is that competitors and spectators must not go on the course area before or during the race – for obvious reasons.

The two major forms of Orienteering as practised in international and championship events are *Point Orienteering* and *Score Orienteering*.

POINT ORIENTEERING

This is a straight race around a circuit of control points. The fastest time decides who is the winner.

The competitor runs or walks around a circuit of controls in a fixed order. Usually the course is in the form of a loop of uneven shape, the finish being close to the start to simplify the officiating. In large championships the start and finish are best separated, sometimes by several miles. Although this means the duplication of organisation and the provision of transport, the competitor has a more challenging course which does not cover the same vicinity twice – once at the beginning and then on return to the finish. This is a real help, for the last section of a course becomes child's play to the expert orienteerer as he immediately recognises the lie of the land on the second visit.

The Point Orienteering event may be found under the title 'Cross-

Country Orienteering'. This is rather vague because the sport of Orienteering as a whole is cross-country. Therefore to be specific and to keep in line with the edicts of the established centres of the sport, 'Point Orienteering' is the accurate description of this event in which half a dozen to a dozen controls make up the course, with a strict control order being decided by the course setter. Competitors must visit the controls in the sequence given, although they are free to choose whatever route they consider best to 'join up' the controls. With manned control points it is easy to check that the right order is being followed by the orienteerer by looking at his control and stamp card. In minor events, where it is not possible to have this manual check, secret instructions can be left at certain controls and general warning given of their presence to the competitor – but not to which specific control they will apply. Taking the controls in incorrect order may benefit a competitor, as in the example of a course shown in Fig. 1. It would be advantageous to 'pick up' No. 6 from No. 2 on the way to No. 3, so enabling the orienteerer to nip across from No. 5 to No. 7. The instruction would therefore be on No. 5 control to stamp '2, 3 or even 4 times at next control'. Thus anyone having already visited No. 6 would have to visit it again.

A good point event will have a cleverly chosen selection of control

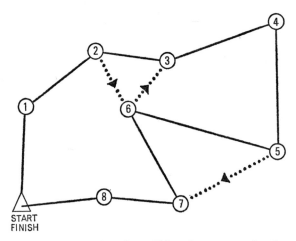

Fig. 1. A course where it could be advantageous for the competitor to take the controls in incorrect order (e.g. from 2 to 6)

29

points between which there will be no easy direct route which everyone will automatically follow. Rather will there be many choices of direct but difficult and indirect but easier routes.

Since the start organisation sends one competitor off at one-minute – or preferably two-minute – intervals, the likelihood of consecutive competitors taking exactly the same course is reduced, and it is possible to run round a course without seeing another person. In Sweden the start is invariably in a heavily-wooded and wild area. I have started into the 'jungle' of the Swedish forest and had this wonderful experience of solitary progress. It is good because there are no other competitors hesitating or running in contradictory directions to disturb one's own concentration. Open heath or any type of country with visibility over twenty yards is unsuitable for the start of the event.

The course for the Point Event for the World Championships in 1966 was already marked on the competitors' maps. The maps were given at the pre-start time and we had three minutes to run or walk one hundred yards to the start and study the map at the same time. However, minor events necessitate the copying of the course by the competitor himself from a master map situated in a leafy grove several hundred yards after the start line along a streamer trail in the forest. Thus skill in speedy, accurate map-marking becomes an essential factor in close competition, for a minute saved at the maps may be the margin between first and second place.

Team Scoring is decided by the addition of the times recorded by the nominated team members – the lowest total indicating the winning team.

The time needed for completing the point event depends on the number of starters. A field of several hundred orienteerers, e.g. three hundred one-minute intervals is equal to a start spread of over five hours, plus the slowest competitors possibly taking three and a half hours, gives a maximum of eight and a half hours! Thus point events need a whole day to complete.

POINT EVENTS—SUMMARY
Course and start: Always in a heavily-wooded area or an area of restricted visibility, because all competitors follow the same 'corridor' across country.

One and a half to ten miles, according to event type.

Controls: Three to fourteen, according to event type.

Strict sequence of Controls in loop or point-to-point.

Master Map method: Competitors mark own maps *after* start – so map-marking counts in race time.

Many hours needed. Not good for novices.

Competitive method: Fastest times having visited all controls correctly.

SCORE ORIENTEERING

This is 'collecting' as many control points as possible within a fixed time. The top scorer is the winner.

As many as thirty control points are scattered over an area of up to five square miles. Each control rates a score, the value depending upon its difficulty and distance from the common start-finish area. Distant or difficult controls can reward the competitor's visit by as many as fifty points, whereas those close to the start may be only worth five or ten points. There tend to be few and widely-scattered high-scoring controls and many low-scoring controls crowding in towards the vicinity of the start and finish.

The time for each competitor is usually one and a half hours from his start. If he returns before the time has elapsed, there is no adjustment to the total of the points he has amassed by visiting as many controls as possible, and his gross score is his final score. However, late return is penalised at the rate of three points per minute (or one point per twenty seconds). If he returns ten minutes late he loses thirty points, so that the late returner's final score is his gross score of points collected less the appropriate deduction for lateness.

An example of a score event result:

	Score	Minutes Late	Penalty	Total
1. K. Carruthers	246	10 min. 20 sec.	31	+215 pts.
2. S. Smith	268	19 min. 10 sec.	58	+210 pts.
3. L. Blinder	208	Early	Nil	+208 pts.
4. K. Knuts	280	30 min.	90	+190 pts.
5. L. Man	188	Early	Nil	+188 pts.
Etc. . . .				
101. N. Chance	48	24 min.	72	− 24 pts.

Team Scoring can be carried out in the following ways:

First Method. Individuals work independently, collecting controls, and members of each team add their scores together – highest totals

31

showing the winning team. This is the best method, for it allows an event to be both team and individual.

Second Method. Here the teams combine to collect all controls, with the best men picking up the farthest and hardest controls and the less competent picking up the easier ones. The team with the highest total wins. For organisers this method is not as satisfactory as the first, since it means more controls spread over a wider area.

The fact that competitors follow any course they wish means that more open ground is quite suitable for score Orienteering. In contrast to the Point event where the sight of other competitors is a help, score competitors fan out in every direction, thus even hindering rather than assisting each other. Therefore a score event organisation can eat up hundreds of competitors and disgorge them in one go for the countryside to soak them up immediately. Thus the score event can be completed in two hours at most if necessary. This makes it fine for summer evenings on the local common.

A score event is, in its own way, more intriguing in that you have to weigh the pros and cons of visiting the control points – balancing the running time necessary with the reward of the score for the particular control point and the tactical 'opening up' of other controls in the vicinity, so giving a bonus of more points for the trip in that direction.

Score events are best designed to suit the majority of the competitors so that those who are novices or slow will only derive satisfaction and experience from the event in visiting adjacent simple controls. The average competitor should have a chance to win by sensible, steady, accurate progress through the mid-range of controls. The expert looks avariciously at the fat prizes offered by distant and difficult controls. In fact, I myself turn a score event into a point event by drawing in my own selected circuit of every single control and race off like a man possessed visiting every control to amass a 100% score. The risk is there, rather like gambling – if you can be 'spot on' all the time you make the finish without penalty, but – and this often happens – if you make one small miscalculation you arrive back late enough to lose out to those steady and sensible competitors who took no risks!

The main difference between the score event and the point event is that in the former the map-copying from the master maps is done *outside* competition time. Fifteen minutes is allowed in the master map room – or the map is supplied at the pre-start, already fully marked up with all the control points, and ten minutes are then available for studying and deciding upon your method of visiting the control points.

It is wise to leave some low-scoring controls close to the finish until the last, since they may be collected last if your time has not quite run out.

Finally, you MUST wear a wrist watch for score events!

SCORE EVENTS—SUMMARY

Course and start: May be in open country or wooded area, since competitors fan out in all directions. Area – one to five square miles.

Controls: Up to thirty as necessary, scattered. Any order of visiting by competitors.

Time limit: One and a half hours (or less).

Competitive method: Highest scores after deduction of any penalties that may apply.

Good for novices and expert alike, and if time available is short.

These two main types of Orienteering may be carried out in other forms.

Point Orienteering may be done in the dark as a night point event, or may be incorporated in a relay race. This relay may be done at night, but is not advisable, as competitors have to wait in the cold for hours for their turn to race.

Score Orienteering may be carried out in the dark as a night score event. This is not often done for safety reasons. In the point event it is possible, within limits, to estimate where someone has been lost when the controls are fully or partly manned. This is not possible in a score event because of the free choice of route. An advantage of night score events is that no 'Indian file' of orienteerers is to be seen trailing across the countryside like a torch procession, as is the case in a night point event.

THE NIGHT EVENT

Obvious differences will exist in the organisation of night events and in the method adopted by the competitors. Usually controls will be sited at very obvious features and in such a way that competitors do not have to negotiate dangerous ground. For the novice and the inexpert the control flags are best lit by a red marker light visible only in the vicinity – about fifteen or twenty yards round the Control Point. For experts a marker flag painted fluorescent red is suitable. It is wise to have some, or preferably all, controls named for safety's sake. The course need not be as long as in the day event – even a third of the distance can be sufficient in English standards of competition unless you, as an organiser, wish to miss a whole night's sleep, having set the field off at 6 p.m. on a winter's evening.

The skill of Scandinavian orienteerers is so great that major night events there show ridiculously fast average speeds. In fact the Scandinavian night champions would beat the best English daytime racers on that basis!

The skills of travelling on a compass direction, pace-counting and map-reading will be called upon and tested to a very high level in the night events.

Juniors, girls and novices must compete in pairs in night events. Only experienced Orienteerers may compete singly. They should take a whistle in case of emergency and understand the recognised distress signals with torch and whistle.

THE RELAY EVENT

This race brings out the best qualities of team and individual competition. Many relay races are held in Scandinavia. One such is a *Tiomila* Relay, which is a 'Ten' Relay, where ten men make up each team and the total distance of the race is ten Swedish miles, equal to sixty-two English miles. The winning time is about fourteen hours, so each orienteer runs for an average of nearly one and a half hours. These races start one day and go right on to the middle of the next. Clearly there is a terrific amount of organisation in such an event, and this can be reduced to a minimum by running the event over several legs. At the 1966 World Championships at Fiskas, Finland, the relay event was organised by Osmo Niemalä, with twenty-one control points spread over twelve square miles.

The relays were made up from selections of these twenty-one controls and made use of three separate start-and-finish areas. The results from all controls were radioed in and spectators were able to watch the progress of the race on visual aids consisting of 'Clothes line results' (see page 53) which were switched up and down to give the order and time of the teams as they fought it out. The Ladies' Event was tremendously exciting, with the result always in doubt until the very end when the Swedish girls' last runner, Gunborg Ahling, crossed the line 2 hr. 42 min. 58 sec. after the start of the first Swedish runner, but only 21 seconds before Haila Hovi of Finland.

As the first leg runners had started at intervals of 1 minute according to a ballot – then it was necessary to rearrange start times for the second leg to produce a straight race. This was arranged by allowing all the first-leg competitors to complete the course. Then the second-leg runners started off at the intervals decided by the times achieved by the first leg runners, i.e.: the fastest team starting first with the other team runners following at the appropriate time intervals that their first-leg runners had finished behind the leader on the first leg. Therefore from the second leg it became a straight race. The lead and order changed many times as fortunes swayed one way and the other between the teams, making an exciting competition for competitors and spectators alike.

The mens' course, first leg of 8.5 Km. was from S (Start) to controls 1, 2, 3, 4, 5, 6, to hand over at V. Chris Brasher ran this leg for the English team and his time was 1 hr. 26 min. 27 sec. The fastest leg was by Finland's Erkki Kohvakka in 56 min. 04 sec. – but he was only 1 second faster than Sweden's Bertil Norman!

The second leg was from the new start point K through controls 7, 8, 9, 10, 11, 12 to finish at V. This made a distance of 8.7 Km. and the fastest time was by Karl Johansson in 55 min. 40 sec., practically a full 5 minutes faster than Finland's Rolf Koskinen! England's Bob Astles took 2 hr. 57 min. 13 sec.

The third leg was from K through 13, 14, 5, 7, 8, 9, 10, 11, 12 to V for a distance of 8.1 Km. Here Sweden's lead in the relay was increased a further five minutes over Finland by Anders Morelius – Sweden's 1966 Champion.

The fourth and final leg of 9.5 Km. was from K through 13, 15, 16, 17, 18, 19, 20, 21, to Z (Finish).

Although Finland's Aimo Tepsell ran 1 hr. 3 min. 36 sec. against Goran Ohlund's (Sweden) 1 hr. 5 min. 22 sec. Sweden raced over line first in 3 hr. 51 min. 42 sec. to win the World Relay Title.

England were eliminated after the first two legs, since Brasher and Astles combined times were more than two hours behind the leader

RESULTS FOR EACH LEG AND THE FINISH IN THE

Final Position	Team	First leg			Second leg				Team Position
		Runner	Leg time	Position	Runner	Leg time	Position	Total time	
1	Sweden	Bertil Norman	56.05	2	Karl Johansson	55.40	1	1.51.45	1
2	Finland	Erkki Kohvakka	56.04	1	Rolf Koskinen	1.00.52	2	1.56.56	2
3	Norway	Dagfinn Olsen	58.05	3	Ola Skarholt	1.02.27	3	2.00.32	3
4	Switzer-land	Alex Schwager	1.04.45	4	Fritz Maurer	1.23.04	7	2.27.04	5
5	Denmark	Flemming Norgard	1.22.05	8	Finn Faxner	1.20.40	6	2.42.45	7
6	Czecho-slovakia	Jindrich Novotny	1.07.00	5	Antonin Urbanec	1.18.40	4	2.25.40	4
7	East Germany	Rolf Heinemann	1.13.27	7	Achim Zemanek	1.29.47	9	2.43.14	8
8	Hungary		1.10.52	6	Ladislaus Deseo	1.28.30	8	2.39.22	6
	Bulgaria	Michail Galov	1.23.14	9	Nikola Bedelev	1.20.34	5	2.43.48	–
	Austria	Frans Trampusch	1.32.02	11	Sepp Michael Pacher	2.22.01	10	3.54.03	
	England (not count-ing)	Chris Brasher	1.26.27	10	Bob Astles	2.57.13	11	4.23.40	

RESULTS FOR EACH LEG AND THE FINISH IN THE

Final Position	Team	First leg			Second leg	
		Runner	Leg time	Position	Runner	Leg time
1	Sweden	Kerstin Granstedt	1.00.28	3	Eivor Steen-Olsson	46.47
2	Finland	Anja Meldo	1.05.12	4	Pirjo Ruotsalainen	52.09
3	Norway	Astrid Hansen	54.07	2	Ragnhild Kristiansen	1.14.50
4	Switzerland	Annakathi Grieder	53.41	1	Irene Kohli	1.23.10
5	East Germany	Ulrike Heinemann	1.09.27	6	Ria Meyer	1.01.43
6	Czecho-slovakia	Ludmila Kumbarova	1.20.11	7	Hadesda Linhartova	52.06
	Denmark	Vibeke Sabye Christiansen	1.08.15	5	Marianne Selbo	55.32
	Hungary	Margrete Babay	1.33.57	8	Barbara Cser (Dropped out)	
	Bulgaria	Olga Taschova (Dropped out after second control)				

TYPES OF RACES

Third leg				Team Posi-tion	Fourth leg				Final Posi-tion
Runner	Leg time	Posi-tion	Total time		Runner	Leg time	Posi-tion	Total time	
Anders Morelius	54.35	1	2.46.20	1	Goran Ohlund	1.05.22	2	3.51.42	1
Juhani Salmenkyla	59.02	2	2.55.38	2	Aimo Tepsell	1.03.36	1	3.59.34	2
Aage Hadler	1.07.46	3	3.08.18	3	Stig Berge	1.18.17	3	4.26.35	3
Max Juni	1.08.53	4	3.36.42	5	Christian Jaggi	1.31.18	5	5.08.00	4
Leif Norgard	1.12.40	6	3.55.25	6	Keld Olsen	1.19.00	4	5.14.25	5
Gustave Bartak	1.09.15	5	3.34.55	4	Svatoslav Galik	1.44.11	8	5.18.06	6
Harald Grosse	1.21.58	7	4.05.12	7	Helmut Conrad	1.36.02	6	5.41.14	7
Georg Schonvissky	1.40.28	9	4.19.60	9	Ivan Skerlets	1.40.43	7	6.00.33	8
Grigor Kaloianov	1.36.00	8	4.19.48	–	Dropped out				
Overran maximum time allowed									
Overran maximum time allowed									

Position	Total time	Team position	Third leg				Final position
			Runner	Leg time	Position	Total time	
1	1.47.15	1	Gunborg Ahling	55.43	4	2.42.58	1
3	1.57.21	2	Haila Hovi	45.48	2	2.43.19	2
6	2.08.57	4	Ingrid Thoresen	45.32	1	2.54.29	3
7	2.16.51	7	Katharina Perch-Nielsen	51.15	3	3.08.06	4
5	2.11.10	5	Erika Wauer	1.17.04	5	3.38.14	5
2	2.12.17	6	Dobruse Novotna	1.37.41	6	3.49.58	6
4	2.03.47	3	Karin Agesen (Missed a control)				

at that stage – and these two English runners had used up nearly 32 minutes more time than the Swedish team's total for four runners!

Relay races can be simplified by adopting the clover-leaf principle where a number of 'legs' are laid out from a common start-and-finish point.

The Finnish method of relieving each competitor of his map enables the re-use of control points, since the secrecy of the course is maintained until the end of the competition. (*Note:* Competitors must not be allowed to have any sight or knowledge of a course until just before the start moments.)

A common start-and-finish with twenty controls scattered around – and a number of selections involving ten controls will simplify organisation – but don't forget to take the maps from the competitors as they finish their leg of the race!

Route Orienteering demands skill in following a marked line (route) through the countryside with secret control points on the route. The competitor who has followed the correct course will be expected to mark these controls on his map, and he is expected to be able to indicate his position exactly. Time has no bearing on this type of event, but a time limit is placed on completion of the course, the winner being the one who has located most controls with the greatest accuracy. Not many competitors can be accommodated in line events, since they must be separated by a reasonable distance to avoid later competitors seeing the earlier starters.

In *Project Orienteering*, a project has to be carried out at the controls. It may be any project suitable to the organiser – for scouts it could be building a campfire, in military circles it might be a test of rifle skill or making a protective construction for survival, but for pure Orienteering it may be the recognition of features in the vicinity of the control by bearings and descriptions.

These last two types of Orienteering are more valuable as training ventures.

CHAPTER THREE

How To Run Orienteering Races—For Competitors and Officials

Orienteering races organised in the British Isles are held under the auspices of the various clubs and associations which are affiliated to the English and Scottish Orienteering Associations and governed by the British Orienteering Federation. All details of current events may be obtained from the offices of these various bodies, as listed in the Appendix, page 107.

The sport of Orienteering is organised to afford competitions up and down the country on practically every weekend of the year, with the exception of high summer when excessive growth on heath or in forest makes it rather difficult and perhaps dangerous to the progress of the orienteerer. Happily this coincides with holiday time in late July and August, although, with the demand for more and more races building up, the slack period is tending to be squeezed smaller every year.

The fixture lists that are now the foundation of the sport are meticulously arranged by the B.O.F. Fixtures Secretary with the co-operation of all concerned in the sport of Orienteering. This country-wide co-operation guarantees that there are no clashes of important events in date or place. Anyone who wishes to organise a race will be well advised to do so within the framework of the established Orienteering organisations, because this will secure the experienced assistance, co-operation and invaluable advice of the groups and individuals who have put the sport on such a sound footing in the British Isles (see list of Clubs and Associations in Appendix, page 107).

For those who wish to organise a race for their own closed group or organisation the advice and guidance contained in this chapter are indispensable. They will enable anyone to organise his own event, provided he has good map-reading ability and the capability of identifying on the ground specific features shown on his map. This may be the main reason for seeking the assistance of experienced Orienteering circles, because one wrongly placed control can ruin an event, or bad organisation can destroy the initial flush of enthusiasm for Orienteering.

For those who have some experience of Orienteering, this chapter offers assistance in simplifying, streamlining and clarifying their event organisation.

While, on the face of it, it would appear that there is an enormous amount of paperwork and organisation needed for an Orienteering event to be promoted efficiently, the general idea is extremely simple and two experienced orienteerers can put on a small event with only two days' notice. Briefly, competitors set off at one-minute intervals to find red control markers located in the countryside. They prove they have visited the controls by stamping a card – in very primitive competitions I have seen girls and boys returning with the set of stamp marks on their forearms and legs! The time they take to go round the course is recorded and the result is there for all to see. That sounds simple and it is – but when you have a race with hundreds of competitors good organisation is essential, and the machinery of the event organisation is clearly and concisely laid out in the following instructions to competitor and official alike.

STAGE ONE

For officials. First select the venue for the event, and since the basic problem in Orienteering is in communication, as outlined earlier, the second step to take is to apply for your fixture date and venue to be accepted on the fixture lists of your area and/or the National fixture lists. This is to be done by 15th July for the following twelve months. Your communication problem will be solved by the

(*Left*) Euro Meeting, Gothenburg 1966. Gordon Pirie finishes second in the first competition. (*Below*) Euro Meeting 1966. Chris Brasher finishes

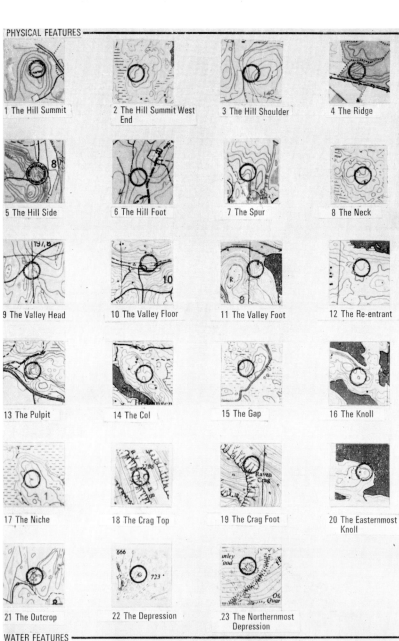

PHYSICAL FEATURES

1 The Hill Summit

2 The Hill Summit West End

3 The Hill Shoulder

4 The Ridge

5 The Hill Side

6 The Hill Foot

7 The Spur

8 The Neck

9 The Valley Head

10 The Valley Floor

11 The Valley Foot

12 The Re-entrant

13 The Pulpit

14 The Col

15 The Gap

16 The Knoll

17 The Niche

18 The Crag Top

19 The Crag Foot

20 The Easternmost Knoll

21 The Outcrop

22 The Depression

23 The Northernmost Depression

WATER FEATURES

24 The Island

25 The Promontory

26 The Stream Junction

27 The Stream and Path Junction

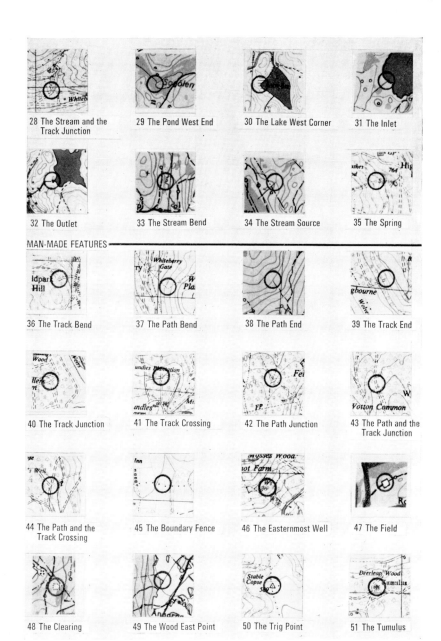

28 The Stream and the Track Junction	29 The Pond West End	30 The Lake West Corner	31 The Inlet
32 The Outlet	33 The Stream Bend	34 The Stream Source	35 The Spring

MAN-MADE FEATURES

36 The Track Bend	37 The Path Bend	38 The Path End	39 The Track End
40 The Track Junction	41 The Track Crossing	42 The Path Junction	43 The Path and the Track Junction
44 The Path and the Track Crossing	45 The Boundary Fence	46 The Easternmost Well	47 The Field
48 The Clearing	49 The Wood East Point	50 The Trig Point	51 The Tumulus

Examples of suitable control points (Figure 2, see Chapter 2, page 46).
The 18 extracts (as listed on page 8) Crown Copyright Reserved

(*Above*) A typical Swedish control – 'By the rock'. (*Below*) 'The lake shore'. No time to waste! An intermediate manned checkpoint

established distribution of these fixture lists. They give details of your event to all concerned, saving you valuable time, work and money: the secretary's name and address, date, venue, type of event, classes, entry fees and procedure and any other relevant information. This will ensure support from Orienteering competitors for your event.

Those who wish to organise an event in the closed group of a club can dispense with official approval but will be well advised to contact the nearest Orienteering organisation to ensure that their proposed event will not clash with a national event. Also they may be able to get the help of experienced Orienteering officials in an advisory or active role.

STAGE TWO

For officials – Initial tasks six weeks before event.

1. Select the exact area for the event.

2. Obtain the landowner's permission for the use of his land for an Orienteering event.

3. Appoint a course setter and course vetter. (The organiser may be the course setter or vetter).

4. First aid arrangements.

5. Recruit officials for organisational tasks on the day.

6. Preliminary refreshment arrangements.

7. Changing facilities.

If possible, radio communication is a great help for safety and spectator interest. Cadet forces, Army units and Mountain Rescue units are helpful in this respect.

The next job for the organiser is to fix the course, and this is dealt with as follows:

COURSE-SETTING AND VETTING

Course-setting and vetting is an art and in the home of Orienteering, Scandinavia, no one can set an Orienteering course until he has reached high standards in all aspects of the sport. This takes years, and so far no one in the British Isles has served sufficient time to be classed as an expert by Scandinavian standards. There are, however, a number of people now reliable at course-setting or vetting in Britain, and we can all learn more, no matter how many years we have to put our hand to any task. This is particularly true in Orienteering.

Course-setting consists of (a) the selection of suitable territory, (b) fixing start and finish arrangements, (c) choice of suitable control points; the order of the control points in the case of Point Orienteering or scoring values in Score events; and marking up the master maps in the last few days before the event.

Course-vetting consists of checking the work of the course-setter in every aspect and checking the master maps on the day of the competition.

One must underline first of all that Orienteering depends entirely on the course-setter and vetter. An entire event may be ruined by one badly placed control. In the present state of early development in Britain of Orienteering, it is essential that the accuracy of the course be guaranteed – checked and double-checked from every angle.

What about the level of difficulty? On the one hand the beginner needs simple controls and he also needs to succeed in events to encourage him to go on. It is *not* advisable to send novices away on a course which, in nine cases out of ten, they cannot hope to complete. Set only an extremely simple course of a few controls within two or three hundred yards from the start point, and allow the novice to 'collect' the controls in any order, as in a score event.

At the other end of the scale the elite orienteerers are being groomed to compete in international races. Therefore the difficulty and length of courses for the 'elite' race have to be set accordingly.

In Scandinavia the terrain is very difficult and physically very demanding. Despite this the elite Swedish Orienteer travels faster than his British contemporaries and maintains his speed over a longer period. Elite competitions need to take between $1\frac{3}{4}$ and 2 hours for the winner. Any course that can be completed in under $1\frac{1}{2}$ hours is not an Elite course, but merely a 'Senior Standard' event.

The officially recommended courses in Britain are as follows, according to age classes:

ALL AGES AS ON THE DAY OF THE COMPETITION

Class	Distance	No. of Controls
Novices (Newcomers)	3 –3½ miles	6–9 controls
B. Boys under 15	1½–2½ ,,	5–9 ,,
G. Girls under 15	1 –2 ,,	4–8 ,,
J.M. Junior men, over 15 and under 18	2½–3 ,,	5–9 ,,
J.W. Junior women, over 15 and under 18	1½–2½ ,,	5–9 ,,
I.M. Intermediate men, over 18 and under 21	3 –3½ ,,	6–9 ,,
I.W. Intermediate women, over 18 and under 21	2½–3 ,,	5–9 ,,
S.M. Senior men, 21 and over	Standard 4 miles	7–10 ,,
	Elite 5½–8 miles	9–14 ,,
S.W. Senior women, 21 and over	3–3½ miles	6–9 ,,
V.M. Veteran men, over 40		
V.W. Veteran women over 40		
Vt.M. Vintage men over 45		
VtW. Vintage Women over 45		

However, if you wish to encourage newcomers, as I have pre-vuously said, do *not* send novices on the type of course recommended above. You will lose them.

The course-setter, therefore, goes about his task within the above limitations, the distances for courses being measured by the most sensible route, not by bee lines across the map.

However, the Elite Standard must be more demanding than officially recommended if British orienteering is to be stimulated to a higher level to justify participation in international competitions. In the final reckoning, the success of the Elite Class in these international competitions will be the stimulant for encouraging youngsters to take up Orienteering.

Course-setters must work with these recommendations for limiting novices and extending elite Orienteerers whenever they set a course, *and* they must encourage criticism and correction by others in order that they may improve their ability.

When several courses are being set embracing all eleven categories, *one* particular condition should be observed. Never send all these eleven classes off to the same first control point or points. The ideal set-up is to send every course off in a different direction to different control points for obvious reasons. Even with several hundred competitors, it is very stupid to have them all converging on the same No. 1 control, as has frequently happened in English Orienteering events. Except for novices the first control should not be a 'gift'. It should involve negotiation of wild countryside for several hundred yards and *not* be located by a road or an outstanding feature or near the changing accommodation, the rendezvous, the pre-start or the finish. Too many courses have tended to be a cross-country run – 'a matter of course' for the first controls. In Sweden, the Elite Course more often than not sends the orienteerer off for a mile through terrible countryside where there are unlimited choices of route and no direct easy one. Late starters should not be able to trot about navigating by the other competitors instead of by their map, and the start list should be made out, within reason, to send the competitors away reasonably spread out. For example, if you have fifty starters, there is no need to get them away within the first hour – spreading them over two hours will be better and provide a greater challenge for every individual.

For championships the field must be limited to a sensible size. Swedish experts inform me that before the advent of selected fields for championship Orienteering races, the winners almost always came from the later starters, who not only have the advantage of seeing other orienteerers but, could also follow the tell-tale tracks near the controls.

These factors all fall within the domain of course-setting and vetting. A course has to be tailored to the competitors and the difficulties matched to them.

What difficulties? It is not feasible to classify Orienteering in this sense. What appears to be difficult on a day when you are overtired may not present a problem on another day when you are perfectly fresh. The fact is that you must find a point on the ground that is shown to you on the map – and this is Orienteering. The course-setter often defeats the purpose of Orienteering by placing the controls in simply-found locations and often in full view of orienteerers in the vicinity who are lost, yet find the control accidentally. This is no use to Orienteering, for the competitor does not have to develop and practise his orienteering skills. A course must ask the competitor to be able to pinpoint his position at all times. Obviously you do not go to the other extreme by hiding the control-marker in a rabbit-hole. It is about right if the control-marker can be seen from a distance of five yards. In difficult courses in Sweden this margin of visibility is often cut down to one yard – for example, when the flag is between two large rocks – but in these cases the feature will tell the good orienteerer to look in the right place.

No, the difficulty in Orienteering is not really concerned with control-marker placing. You must learn to find a control-marker by intelligence in direction-finding, pace-counting and map-reading.

The difficulty factor, which the course-setter varies, is the physical difficulty of the course. If he simplifies control-point locations he removes the true elements of the sport. So course-setters vary the difficulties presented to the physique – keeping the mental problems on a high plane except for novices.

We have already covered the points about terrain selection, so there now follows the question of what features you select.

In Scandinavia, the accepted method that has become established in 99 per cent of controls selected is to use features that *are shown* on the map in the form of specific map symbols. They may be actual physical features in relation to the contour lines and other physical features on the map, e.g. hollows, pits, etc., or they may be man-made features – paths, fences, fire-breaks, buildings, fields and so on – but they must be clearly marked on the map. Any feature only on the ground is not used as a control location unless it is added accurately to the competition map. My friend the Finnish Gold Medal course-setter was aghast at many controls in our first English races, because the use of features on the ground that were non-existent on the map was not correct by Scandinavian methods. Thus, the control used in England which has been described by using 'a' before the description because it is not on the map – 'a path' as distinct from 'the path' – is to be avoided. The distinction that is made by the 'the' prefix is that the feature being used for the control exists on the map. If the course-setter is forced to use features not marked on the map then the 'a' prefix will apply.

The method of describing controls is as follows:

EXAMPLES OF SUITABLE CONTROL POINTS
(Each of the following features, as marked on the map, is illustrated in Fig. 2, between pages 40–41).

1. The Hill Summit
2. The Hill Summit W. End
3. The Hill Shoulder
4. The Ridge
5. The Hill Side
6. The Hill Foot

7. The Spur
8. The Neck
9. The Valley Head
10. The Valley Floor
11. The Valley Foot
12. The Re-entrant
13. The Pulpit
14. The Col
15. The Gap
16. The Knoll
17. The Niche
18. The Crag Top
19. The Crag Foot
20. The Easternmost Knoll
21. The Outcrop
22. The Depression
23. The Northernmost Depression
24. The Island
25. The Promontory
26. The Stream Junction
27. The Stream and the Path Junction
28. The Stream and the Track Junction
29. The Pond West End
30. The Lake West Corner
31. The Inlet
32. The Outlet
33. The Stream Bend
34. The Stream Source
35. The Spring
36. The Track Bend
37. The Path Bend
38. The Path End
39. The Track End
40. The Track Junction
41. The Track Crossing
42. The Path Junction
43. The Path and the Track Junction
44. The Path and the Track Crossing
45. The Boundary Fence
46. The Easternmost well
47. The Field
48. The Clearing
49. The Wood East Point
50. The Trig Point
51. The Tumulus

Notes: Obviously there are many other features which may be used for control markers, such as the Bridge, the Pump, the Quarry, the Marsh, the Rock, etc.

Where a feature extends over more than about ten metres, it is necessary to specify on what part of the feature the control is located by the compass, e.g. North – South-East, plus the word 'most' as in examples 20 and 46 above.

Difference between field and clearing: a field is marked by a boundary and a growing crop, while a clearing is small – about thirty to fifty metres across – without a boundary.

Boundaries may be fences, ditches, dykes, walls or hedges. In control No. 45, the description clearly indicates the type of boundary. This is the correct method of describing boundaries.

CONTROL TERMINOLOGY AND DEFINITION OF FEATURES

(1) Controls shall be marked on the master map by *red* circles of $\frac{1}{2}$ cm. in diameter. The situation of the control shall be in the exact centre of the circle *but* not indicated by a dot or any visible mark. (See Fig. 2).

(2) Controls are numbered on the master maps, and for point events controls are joined with straight red lines to clarify the control order. (See map facing page 88).

The next consideration is to choose the control points in relation to each other so as to present the Orienteerer with a choice of routes between the controls and yet not offer one easy and almost direct route that all will automatically follow.

Terrain will be the governing factor in making the decisions on control sequence. Where possible, a prominent change in ground level and shape is the best obstacle to direct traverse between control points. A large valley, a steep hill, a small mountain, a lake, a river or a marsh are good obstacles to place across the orienteerer's direct path by clever control selection. Even a stretch of rough gorse and heather, with uncertain going underfoot, will present the orienteerer with the need to make a decision between running directly on in a beeline or taking a circuitous route across easier ground or along paths.

The rise and fall of the ground is the greatest deterrent to the direct route, and a rise of one contour (25 feet) can be equal to racing 100 metres round a flat path. If the hill you have to cross is 300 feet high and the direct route across only measures 900 metres, you must not fall into the trap of believing that the direct route is quicker than racing twice as far round the hill on a flat path. Why? Because while you stagger upwards 300 feet (12 contours), involving a horizontal progression of 450 metres to the summit, the fellow racing round the flat will cover 100 metres for every contour level you climb up in addition to your horizontally measured progress of 450 metres. So the climber covers 450 metres plus 1,200 metres, that is 1,650 metres – over a mile! Yet he has only travelled 450 metres to the top of the hill! In addition, the man on the level route is not as tired whereas the climber still has to descend 300 feet – again very demanding on the physique.

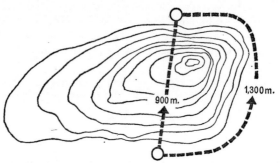

Fig. 3. The longest way home can sometimes be the shortest way home!

Allowing for hazards, let us say one descends at the same speed as the man runs on the level. The climber has then covered 1,650 metres plus his down route of 450 metres in horizontal terms, totalling the equivalent of 2,100 metres of level running. The runner keeping to the level circuitous route had only 1,300 metres to run. (See Fig. 3).

Other considerations come into this choice – it may be easier to orienteer over the hill. The circuitous route may be very difficult underfoot – the paths marked may not be there either! Personally, unless the beeline is ridiculously impassable, I always take it unless there is a fairly direct path involving only a small deviation.

Control points should be chosen to avoid doglegs on the course, and be placed so that outgoing competitors do not give away the control position to incoming ones.

A control should also be placed away from very prominent features, since a big target close to the control (that is, 50–100 metres away) will reduce the problem of finding the flag to a simple matter of running full pelt to the prominent feature (road, lake or steep hill) and spotting the control from there. The control placed 150–350 metres away will demand orienteering skill, during the last metres to the control.

Lastly, the areas that the competitors are liable to cross should be

48

free of dangerous or private ground. If there are such areas they will always be given to the competitor before the start on a 'hazard map' and the competitor blocks them out as 'out of bounds'. The course-setter inspects the terrain at and around the control-points to ensure that his choice is suitable. The terrain must be safe, the growth penetrable without danger, visibility must be right and the control point must satisfy all the criteria laid down.

When you have chosen the control-points on the map, using these criteria, then you are ready to do the practical work involved in course-setting.

FOR THE COMPLETE RULES FOR SETTING ORIENTEERING COURSES PLEASE SEE CHAPTER 8 (page 97). These rules were worked out at the Scandinavian Course-Setters' Conference in Stockholm, 3rd and 4th December, 1966.

After several visits to the terrain to study the suitability of the features for the course – usually three or more visits of three to four hours' careful work – the controls are chosen on the basis of the criteria set out (according to *Barnläggningsnormer*) in this chapter and Chapter 8. Once the control-markers and the start and finish have been decided upon, the course-setter goes out on the course marking every control-point with a strip of brightly-coloured adhesive tape on a convenient tree branch or suitable object. The course-vetter then takes the master map from the course-setter and independently checks all the control-points very carefully. When he is completely satisfied he passes the course. On the day of the competition, course-setter and vetter ensure that the control flags are correctly placed.

The course-vetter's last task, on the morning of the race well before start time, is to check that the start, the finish and all control-points on every master map are accurate and correctly marked. No discrepancy whatsoever must exist between these markings and the location of the control-points and start and finish.

This leaves only the remaining organisational work, details of which now follow. Note that the start and finish points are decided before the control points are selected and confirmed.

ORGANISATION

In the last weeks before the event, entries are flowing in. Generally entries close two weeks before the event.

Only now can you enter the final phase of paperwork. You know the number of entries and therefore it is now possible to duplicate your documents in the right number, avoiding shortage or waste.

For competitors – 3 weeks before event. Enter as per details on Fixture List.

For officials – 2 weeks before event.
Final Phase
(1) Reproduce (a) Maps.
                  (b) Stamp control cards.
                  (c) Clue description sheets.
                  (d) Recorder's sheets.
                  (e) Competitors' instruction cards.
                  (f) Officials' instruction cards.

(2) Check supply of spare compasses.

(3) Complete refreshment arrangements.

(4) Transport arrangements if necessary.

(5) Check changing facilities.

(6) Complete first aid arrangements.

(7) Results Boards.

(8) (a) Competitors' numbers.
     (b) Coloured crêpe paper for streamers for start/finish.
(9) Control markers – make or borrow.

All the paperwork and detail under (1a–f) of the final phase is quite bulky and tiresome, so for the assistance of the organiser the following pages show clearly and concisely how you go about it.

The nominal entry fees (five shillings or less) are to cover the expense of producing this documentary part of Orienteering races.

FOR OFFICIALS: DOCUMENTATION

(1a) MAPS. You need one black and white copy per competitor entered, plus a reasonable number of spares and four to eight master map copies for each course being provided for by the event. For details of copying and use of maps, see Appendix iv.

(1b) STAMP CONTROL CARDS. One per competitor. These will be filled out by the official when entries have closed and handed to competitors on the day of the event.

(1b) STAMP CONTROL CARD

	Hrs.	Mins.	Secs.
Start No. ....Finish Time			
Class.................................Start Time			
Club/School........................Time Taken			
Name ....*Penalty			
*Score			
Position			

*Delete for Pt. Events

1	2	3	4	5	6
7	8	9	10	11	12

(1c) CLUE DESCRIPTION SHEET. One per competitor. For score events the right-hand column including map references – not essential. (For details of control designations, see 'Maps', Chapter 5, page 79).

Control No.	Description	Score
1	The Bend in the Track	
2	The Re-Entrant	
3	On a Stream	
4	The Pulpit	
5	On the Ridge	
6	The Niche	
7	The Path Junction	
8	Between the Depressions	
9	The Clearing	
10	The Trig Point	
11	The Island	
12	The Hill Summit	
13	Finish	

(1d) RECORDERS' SHEETS. One set of sheets per class starting in the event. These sheets are completed on receipt of last entries. The leading competitors should be seeded and balloted for first. Then the remaining starting times chosen by ballot. Duplicate these sheets, one copy for each of the following: (a) Rendezvous, (b) 'Check-In' official, (c) Pre-Start official, (d) Start official, (e) Finish official, (f) for the benefit of competitors, exhibited for reference at Rendezvous and Changing Accommodation.

Start Time	Name	Team	Start Time	Finish Time or Check	Time Taken	Position

(1e) COMPETITORS' INSTRUCTION CARDS (postcards). One per competitor and sent off one week before the event.

Nutfielders Point Orienteering
June 20, 1982

Venue: Cling School, Shropsley.
A327814 10 miles South
of Church Strapsley.
Your Start Time is: 11.48
Class: Elite

Report at least 30 mins. before
your start time. Good Luck.
First control will be removed at
2.30 p.m.

(1f) OFFICIALS' INSTRUCTIONS. Use the same postcard as for competitors and add a brief note of the official's function and location at the event, and the time he is expected to arrive on the day.

When the instructions have been posted off to officials and competitors, the organiser is free to check that all is in order with refreshments, transport between start and finish, changing accommodation and first aid arrangements. This leaves three other Orienteering aspects to deal with, namely results boards, competitors' numbers and control markers.

FOR OFFICIALS

Results Boards. A well-organised event will show the progress of the competitors at various controls as well as the finish time. Times are shown on visual aids at the finish for the benefit of spectators. The easiest way to do this is to string up wires ('clothes-line') between convenient trees and hang boards on them which show a competitor's elapsed time, name and club, e.g.

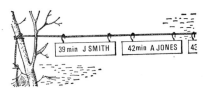

Fig. 4. A 'clothes line' results board, which can be strung between trees

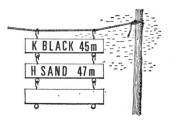

Fig. 5. The 'vertical ladder' results board

A vertical ladder is another variation but is not as good as the 'clothes-line' above. In a ladder result, the name-boards must have 'eyes' on the bottom edge and the results hang vertically, but they can be extremely annoying as they often fall apart.

A blackboard may be used for smaller events.

Competitors' numbers. These are not always necessary, but they are essential in big events for ease of identification at controls and at the finish.

Control-markers. If you are unable to borrow these markers, they can quite easily be made from a round plastic container, twelve inches high (Fig. 6).

Paint it bright red, leave a diagonal white stripe on it and annotate it with a white letter or number. Hang self-inking stamps from the neck of the bottle, the stamps bearing the same code number or letter as that marked on the bottle.

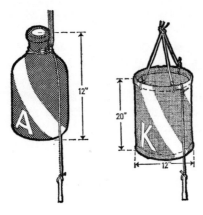

Fig. 6 & 7. (*Left*) A home-made control marker. The round plastic container is painted as described in the text. (*Right*) A tubular marker

Flags between 18 in. and 24 in. may be used, but cylindrical markers held in shape by stiff wire round the top and bottom are the most suitable and should measure 20 in. high by 12 in. in diameter (Fig. 7). These tubular markers are the best-shaped ones because the marker flag is visible from all directions. Colours – red and white diagonal stripes. Hang self-inking stamps from the top edge of the flag – the code letter or number the same on the flag and stamp.

These markers are suspended at the control sites so that they are visible at an appropriate distance from the control (see Chapter 8, page 98, section on course-setting). Control-markers which have no self-inking marking stamp attached necessitate competitors carrying pen or pencil to copy the control key on to their stamp cards.

Now all your organisation is completed except for the day before and the day of the race.

PENULTIMATE DAY

For Competitors. Gather kit (see page 87), check start time and place, make sure you arrive early on competition day.

For officials. Mark four to eight master maps for each of the courses in the event (for details see 'course-setting', page 41). Put them in waterproof coverings (polythene bags are best) and pin to boards which should be large enough to permit the competitor to rest his own map on and copy the course out. Put up road signs to direct arriving competitors to the changing and start areas.

RACE DAY

Competitors start early! All *officials* synchronise their watches with second hand of master clock at start.

Control-markers. The control-markers are placed at the control-points and the key lettering on each control noted so that officials have a copy of the correct letter or number key in each case. The competitors' control cards are then checked with these keys when each competitor's control card is received at the finish.

This placing of control-flags must be completed with plenty of time to spare before the first competitor is due to start. In my estimation one hour should be allowed, so finish control-marking by 9 a.m. This will mean a 7 a.m. start for most courses, unless you have many helpers who can be trusted to locate the control-markers accurately.

The officials and radio men who are to man the controls should be taken to their positions as the control flags are laid. Experience has shown that this is the only safe way to ensure that officials reach the controls and do not get lost themselves!

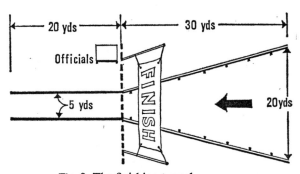

Fig. 8. The finishing tunnel

FINISH TUNNEL

Constructed with rope and clearly displayed, as in Fig. 8.

Two officials record each competitor's number. Two officials record each competitor's time both on a start list and on the competitor's control stamp card. Calculation can then be made of the competitor's race time, checked by the two sets of figures.

If possible an amplifier and loudspeaker is used to keep spectators and finishers informed of progress and the runners' finishing. A radio link with the last control – usually 400 metres or so from the finish – will give advance information on the competitors' arrival. This will make the finish exciting for the spectators and all involved.

START AND FINISH
For officials

Start. Streamers are laid from the rendezvous to the pre-start (if applicable, see chart on page 58), onwards to the start and finally to the master maps. An area by the pre-start will be indicated by signs and streamers as a warm-up area.

For competitors

Maps. Competitors will receive a copy, usually in black and white, of the area of the race at the pre-start. A good tip is to line heavily the grid N–S lines and, in red ballpoint, mark broad arrows to show the north side of the map. You will copy the course controls on to your map from the master maps, which are about 200 to 400 metres from the start.

Stamp control card. You will receive one copy of this card as you check in at the rendezvous. This is your 'passport' for the competition and loss of it will eliminate you. Attach it to the reverse side of your map-case with two strips of adhesive tape without covering the stamp squares, for it is in these squares that you must stamp or write the control designation at each control-point on the course. On completion of the course, even if you fail to find all or any of the controls, you must always return your 'control and stamp card' to the finish officials so that missing competitors may be accounted for.

Clue sheets or control description sheets. You will receive one copy of this at the check-in as well as the control stamp card. You will need to refer to your clue sheet all the time round the course, so put it in your map case where it will keep dry. Another tip is to mark every even-numbered control description on the clue sheet with red ballpoint and clearly write the appropriate number on the right side next to the written description. This makes possible instant reference to the control description you have reached even when you are running full tilt through the forest If you have time, it is a good policy

(*Above*) The beautiful lake shows where we are on our maps. (*Below*) It looks easy – but this long distance competition demands skilled map reading to save valuable energy

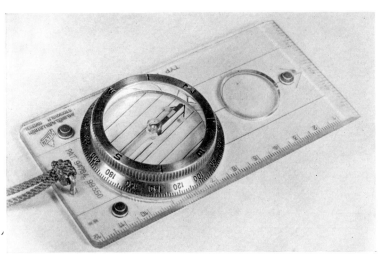

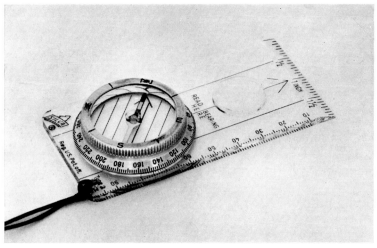

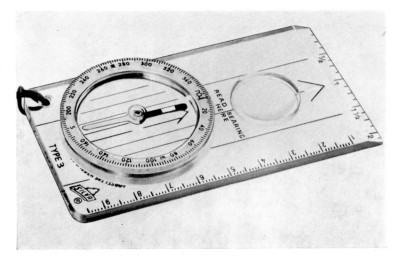

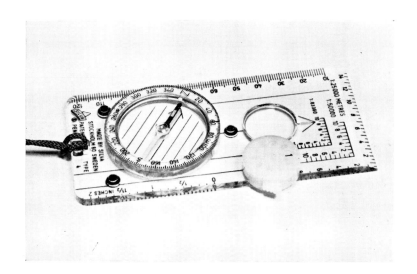

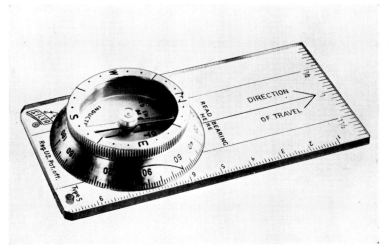

(*Top left*) THE SILVA COMPASS, Type 1. The experts' instrument – very speedy thanks to the fine induction damping of the needle. (*Middle left*) Type II. The silver champion's friend, again with superb damping. (*Bottom left*) Type III. A fine alternative model, liquid filled for a steady needle. (*Above top*) Type IV. The latest model for club champions, with click counter for distance measuring. (*Above*) Type V. The beginner's aid, robust and simple

We always look for a finish which has special qualities for both spectators and competitors to appreciate

When the moment of truth is upon us. Goran Ohlund nears the finish

to memorise all the control descriptions before starting, for this will save even more time during the race.

The rendezvous is usually the changing accommodation, and where convenient the pre-start will be close by in the forest. The start may be between 200 metres to a kilometre (a map square) further away. The master maps will be situated another 100 yards away in the country, together with the box for competitors' pens to be thrown into as they depart after copying the course on to their map.

Finish

This again will be close to the rendezvous, or changing accommodation, and streamers will run from the final control-marker on the course to the finish line. This is usually a distance of about 200–400 yards and in clear ground – across a field or park – so that spectators may cheer on the competitors in their last sprint to the finish line, which itself will be clearly marked with a banner.

The officials who are organising the start and finish will put out these streamers in a few minutes and have everything spick and span at 9.30 a.m., with half an hour left to the first start time at 10.01 a.m.

Officials

One set of officials will have been allocated to each of the following tasks, informed by means of the official's instruction postcards. Each official is also issued with a copy of the recorders' start sheets. Their responsibilities are as indicated below.

(1) *Rendezvous officials* check off the arrival of competitors on the appropriate recorders' sheet; issue the completed control and stamp cards, clue sheets, numbers and loan compasses if necessary. They also accept the entry fees that have not already been paid. A list and box will be available here for competitors to write names and addresses on envelopes and pay postage for copies of results to be sent to them after the race.

(2) *Pre-start officials* give a copy of the map to competitors holding the completed control and stamp cards and numbers. Here any special instructions will be issued on 'out-of-bounds' areas or the country code. Any hazards will also be brought to the notice of competitors.

At approximately ten minutes before start times the competitors are sent by whistle blast on to the start, following the streamers – 200–1,000 metres. This time is treble-checked by (a) the official's

TABLE SHOWING

Area	Rendezvous/ changing room	Pre-start		Start
OFFICIALS	Check in competitors against recorders' sheet	Direct to warm-up area		Hold competitors and dispatch at exact start times by whistle blast
	Issue: Control card Numbers Clue sheets Compass if necessary Take names Entry fees if applicable Addresses for results Vetter checks master maps	Give maps, special Instructions Dispatch by whistle blast at one-minute intervals approximately ten minutes before start time		
COMPETITORS		Drive if two miles. Walk if 100 metres	200/400 metres Streamers. Walk at one minute intervals	Wait for start whistle
	Change Long slacks and long-sleeved jersey Collect wits and equipment Collect compass, map-case and red ballpoint Check in Pay entry if not already done Receive: (1) Clue descrip- tion sheet (2) Stamp control card Stick them on and in map-case Memorise clues Sign up for results service Check you have compass and red ballpoint	Be ready here in time, fifteen minutes before your start time Collect your map as you are dispatched	Walk to start point Follow streamers Study map. Mark grid N/S and mark North of map with red ink	*Waiting Competitors:* Final check of equipment Map/Map-case Compass Red ballpoint

RACE ACTIVITIES

On course			Finish		
Officials manning controls check competitors' numbers Radio times to finish			Record details of finishers	Give refreshments First-aid post	P R I Z E S R E S U L T S

200/400 metres Follow Streamers to master maps	Master maps	Find course controls	Final control 200/400 metres Streamers	Finish line	Refresh-ments	Changing Accommo-dation Showers
RUN with map and red ballpoint at the ready	Copy course *meticulously* Leave pen in bin provided	GO GO Stamp control card when you find controls	S P R I N T	Surrender control card and loaned equipment		

copy of the recorders' sheet, (b) the competitor's control and stamp card and (c) his start number.

(3) *Start officials* send the orienteerers off at their precise start times by whistle blast. This is the true start of the race and the competitor is now using race time. He runs the 100 metres or so along the streamers to the master maps and finds his course map. An official may be on duty to help direct here, but this is not essential.

(4) *Control Officials:* When possible, every control will be manned, and the officials who do this job must not reveal their presence or that of the control to the competitors, so it is advisable for them to wear dark clothing that merges with their surroundings and position themselves accordingly.

Finish Officials

At the finish line the competitor surrenders his control card (and loaned compass if applicable). The official records his finishing time on it, checking that all the control stamps have been collected correctly and also noting the details on his copy of the recorders' sheet. Those responsible for updating the results system do so as competitors finish and keep intermediate information boards up to date if radio information is being passed back from controls.

Refreshments should be offered here at the finish.

CLEARING UP

The first control will be removed at a predetermined time, usually about 2.30 p.m. for 10 a.m. starts. The rest will be removed in order at appropriate intervals during the afternoon. All streamers and any rubbish must be cleared up, so leaving the countryside as you would wish to find it. The final results should be read out and prizes given at the changing accommodation.

Results sheets will be printed as quickly as possible after the event and circulated to those who filled in the results service list.

FINALLY

Write letters of thanks to all those who made the event possible.

CHAPTER FOUR

The Compass

This chapter is divided into two distinct parts:

First – *Orienteering with a compass*, which helps the orienteerer to learn how to use his compass almost instantly. He must then practise for perfection.

Second – *Academic Points*, which gives a short background and explanation of the details of the compass. These are mostly irrelevant to the champion orienteerer, but nevertheless cannot be ignored altogether in dealing with the compass.

ORIENTEERING WITH A COMPASS

Working with your protractor-type Orienteering compass is essentially simple in practice, despite the complications involved. The following paragraphs will teach you how to become confident with your compass, and enable you to negotiate an Orienteering course accurately and with the minimum of time wasted on compass work.

Practical use of the compass in Orienteering races is confined to the following three drills:

(1) *Finding your direction of travel*, called taking a bearing. Needed for about 90% of the race. A bearing can be taken in three to four seconds.

(2) *Measuring of distance*. This is done during 90% of the race and takes only a couple of seconds.

(3) *Finding your Location*. This is called Resections and is done if uncertain of your position. It takes from thirty seconds to one minute.

Before learning how to carry out these three drills, you need a good knowledge of the construction and markings of the Orienteering compass, and one piece of technical knowledge: what the Magnetic Variation is and how it has to be taken into account.

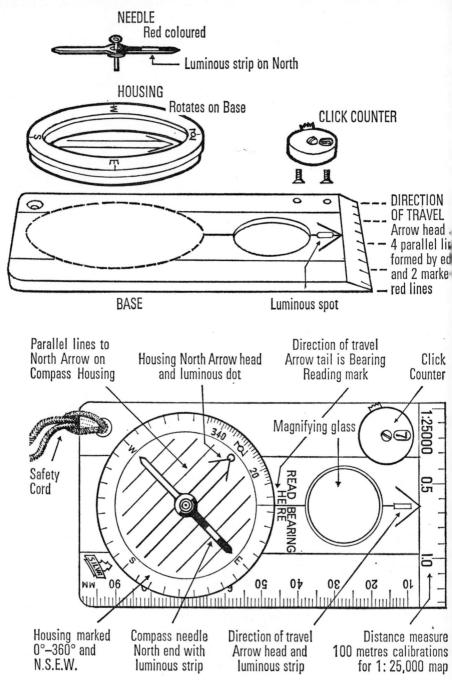

NEEDLE
Red coloured
Luminous strip on North

HOUSING
Rotates on Base

CLICK COUNTER

DIRECTION OF TRAVEL
Arrow head
4 parallel lines formed by edge and 2 marked red lines

BASE

Luminous spot

Parallel lines to North Arrow on Compass Housing

Housing North Arrow head and luminous dot

Direction of travel Arrow tail is Bearing Reading mark

Click Counter

Magnifying glass

Safety Cord

READ BEARING HERE

Housing marked 0°–360° and N.S.E.W.

Compass needle North end with luminous strip

Direction of travel Arrow head and luminous strip

Distance measure 100 metres calibrations for 1 : 25,000 map

Fig. 9. Exploded and plan view of a Type 3 Silva Compass

The Orienteering compass is used in the form of the protractor-type Silva Compass in various models from simple to sophisticated. These were invented and developed by the Kjellström family of famous Swedish orienteerers.

Fig. 9 is an exploded and plan view of a Type 3 Silva Compass which has the basic layout and components of all Orienteering compasses.

The main points, which must be learned by heart and are instantly recognised and used almost instinctively by the experienced orienteerer, are:

A. The direction of travel arrow (with luminous strip for the night orienteerer) Fig. 10. This you see on the protractor baseplate of the compass. Note the two adjacent parallel lines, together with the parallel long edges of the baseplate. These are the lines we use constantly to set the compass in the *direction of travel* on the map – that is, from your location at any time on to your next destination, which is usually the next control-point. The tail of the *direction of travel arrow* is the mark for reading a bearing (unnecessary) and *applying magnetic variation* (necessary).

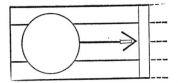

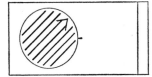

Fig. 10. Silva Compass—
Direction of Travel
arrow

Fig. 11. Silva Compass—
Compass housing arrow-
head

B. Compass housing arrowhead (with luminous dot for the night orienteerer) Fig. 11. Marked on the base of the compass housing together with six parallel red lines. On the expensive compass the compass housing is clear, allowing the map to be read through it. Thus the lines can be aligned with the map-grid lines for the purpose of taking a bearing. The circumference rim of the housing is calibrated 0°–360° for bearings which are read off at the tail of the *direction of travel arrow* on the circumference of the rim of the housing (unnecessary) and *where you make adjustment for magnetic variation* (necessary).

C. Compass needle, painted red at the North end with luminous strip for the night Orienteerer, Fig. 12. Always points *North.*

NB Care! If yours doesn't you are at the North or South Pole – or *you are standing on magnetic ground or a steel bridge.*

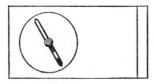
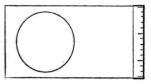

Fig. 12. Silva Compass—
Compass needle

Fig. 13. Silva Compass—
Distance measure

D. Distance Measure. Calibrated for 100 metres on Ordnance Survey 1/25000 (2½ in. to mile) maps. Fig. 13. Merely place scale on map along *direction of travel* to be measured and read off estimating parts of 100 metres that might apply.

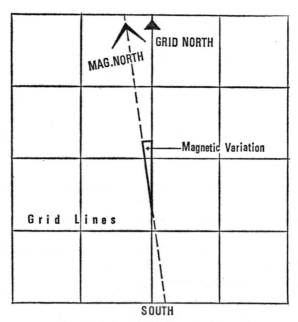

Fig. 14. Calculating the magnetic variation

MAGNETIC VARIATION

This technical point describes the small angle of difference between the North indicated by the grid lines on your map and the Magnetic North indicated by the compass needle. This is a fact and the Magnetic Variation is at present between 6° and 9° West for the British Isles. The margins round maps tell in words and diagramatically what Magnetic Variation is applicable. For further 'whys' and 'wherefores' the second part of this chapter should be consulted. (See Fig. 14.)

You must know the Magnetic Variation for (a) finding direction of travel, and (b) finding position.

Once you have learned these points on the compass and Magnetic Variation, you are ready to learn the three compass drills necessary in Orienteering.

(1) FINDING YOUR DIRECTION OF TRAVEL

Practically throughout an Orienteering race we are going to be concerned with what direction to take, and a typical course will call for following up to thirty, and even forty, directions of travel, stopping only for a few seconds or, when you are more skilled, making the adjustments of compass from your map as you run at speed.

But you cannot run before you can walk! Here are the three steps for finding your direction of travel and putting it into practice together with the measured distance: (see IV).

(i) Place compass on map, long edge along *direction of travel*, as indicated (Fig. 15).

(ii) Twist compass housing until arrowhead is parallel with map-grid lines, as indicated (Fig. 16). *Disregard compass needle!*

(iii) . . . and twist housing *anti-clockwise* to allow for Magnetic Variation (Fig. 17). In this example the 8° is read off at direction of travel arrow tail. *Still disregard compass needle!* Compass is now set.

NB From now on you do not touch compass housing until a new bearing is to be taken.

Next action is to measure for distance.

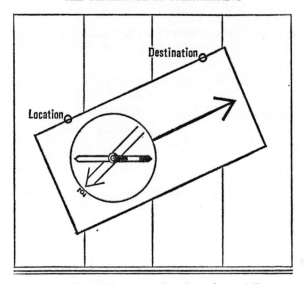

Fig. 15. Finding your direction of travel (i)

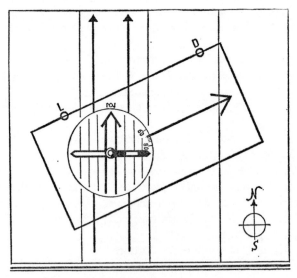

Fig. 16. Finding your direction of travel (ii)

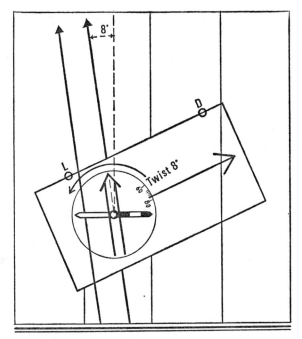

Fig. 17. Finding your direction of travel (iii)

(2) MEASURING YOUR DISTANCE

This is usually done immediately after finding direction of travel (stage iii). Place the measuring scale at the end of the compass on the course from location to destination and read off the distance (Fig. 18). Then you apply the direction of travel as follows (remembering the distance you have just measured!).

From now on the compass needle is used.

FINDING YOUR DIRECTION OF
TRAVEL (Continued)

(iv) *Final Practical Step.* Hold compass in right hand, swivel round until compass needle agrees with compass housing arrowhead (North to North, for goodness' sake!). See Fig. 19.

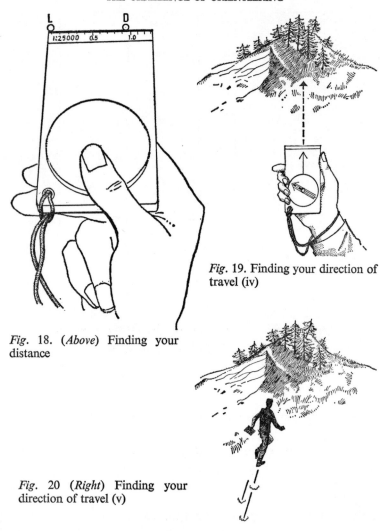

Fig. 19. Finding your direction of travel (iv)

Fig. 18. (*Above*) Finding your distance

Fig. 20 (*Right*) Finding your direction of travel (v)

(v) Take sighting on a feature, run to it counting double steps (right or left foot striking the ground). Repeat compass sighting when you have reached the feature. In thick bush, constant reference to compass is necessary. See Fig. 20. Experience pays handsomely in this drill. Continue until you reach destination, having counted appropriate number of steps.

To complete *Measuring distance* it is necessary to elaborate on double pacing.

In measuring distance we count double paces and step-counting is an art in itself. You need experience to apply it and to learn not to rely on it for absolute accuracy. Why? Because the length of one's step alters according to intrinsic and extrinsic factors. Taking myself as an example, I start off very fresh and need only twenty-four double steps for 100 metres on a footpath. Now I leave the path and run across a rough heath – fifty steps to 100 metres. Cross a marsh, seventy steps to 100 metres – but it was only seventy-two metres across! Go up a very steep hill, 100 steps to 100 metres. The hill is 242 metres long! Eventually I return, after one and a half hours, towards the finish and run along the footpath I started on. It is slow now – and it is a cheat because I take forty-eight steps for the 100 metres! Fatigue!

The answer is, of course, to have a computer or slide rule, do the hundreds of calculations necessary and finish two hours after everyone else. It's a joke? Not really, but it proves conclusively that you must measure how far your *travel distance* is in *metres* and use your experience to estimate what the number of paces you are taking really means. Even then, the skill of reading the map and the terrain round you will be the best criterion to use – checked by step-counting to the nearest ten metres.

To use a scale on your compass of so many steps to the distance travelled, thus choosing a fixed number of steps to each 100 metres, would be fatal. Ninety per cent of the time it is wrong and you will not even know which is the ten per cent when the steps are correct. So stick to measuring distance and follow your own flexible application of step-counting based on experience. For this purpose it is good to go out into the countryside, try measuring distances on different types of terrain and practise pace-counting.

A GENERAL GUIDE FOR 100 METRES PACING

	FRESH	TIRED		FRESH	TIRED
Fast path	24	48	Downhill	20	40
Rough ground	40	60	Marsh	120	200
Uphill	80	100	Rocks	100	150

To relieve you of some brainwork a click counter (tachometer) can be fitted to your compass and this is useful when you have to cover sections of over 300 or 400 metres. Most courses have a long leg of a mile or so, and it is quite easy to slip up in counting fourteen or so groups of 100 metres. (Each grid square of your $2\frac{1}{2}$ in. map is 10 by 100 metres (1 kilometre).

ORIENTATING THE MAP

Another skill which ties in with compass work is map orientation – that is pointing the North (top edge) of your map towards the North indicated by the compass. This enables you to look at the map and the land about you and agree every feature and direction. A lake on your right will be on the right of the map as you look at it. A house on the hill in front of you will be at the top end of your map, and a monument on your left will be on the left side of your map as you look at it. Simply speaking, if you are running North then you are holding the map with the North away from you at the top.

In Orienteering I am moving at all times on my direction of travel given by my compass. I hold my map horizontal in my left hand, automatically orientated (set) because I am 'running down' the same line on the map as on the ground. I don't like holding the map vertically unless running up a cliff. It isn't logical – so keep it horizontal! If I turn a corner I turn my map in my hand accordingly so keeping it orientated at all times. To make for easy map-reading, I keep my left thumb beside my location, moving it from feature to feature as I progress. This ensures constant double-checking of my location, aided by pace-counting. Thus I never go through an elaborate process of orientating my map directly by my compass. However, this is done in a classroom situation by the following steps:

First: Twist compass housing until Magnetic Variation is set on it – Magnetic Variation, in this example, is 8°. See Fig. 21.

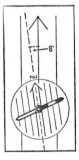

Fig. 21. Orientating the map—stage one

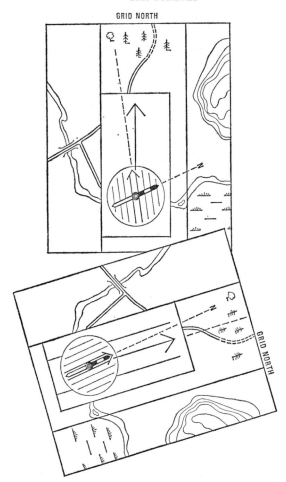

Figs. 22 & 23. (*Top*) Orientating the
map—stage two (*Bottom*) stage three

Second: Put compass on map (with map flat and horizontal) and
the direction of travel arrow along a North/South (vertical) grid
line agreeing North to North end of map. See Fig. 22.

Third: Rotate map with compass resting on it in a horizontal plane
until the compass needle and the compass housing arrowhead
coincide. Map is now orientated or 'set'. See Fig. 23.

71

One can see how much time I save when Orienteering by cutting out the above. Actually, if you are lost, a simple method of approximate orientating ('setting') your map is to look at the compass needle and agree the map with it-North towards North, which is done with no disturbance of your direction of travel compass-setting. The small Magnetic Variation and visual error must, of course, be left out of account.

Your last lesson in the compass drills is:

(3) *Finding your location.* When you are uncertain of your location, you take bearings on two distinctive landmarks at about 90° to each other, and sometimes a third to treble check. If you were completely lost you would not recognise any landmark, but this situation hardly ever happens to a good orienteerer because he is constantly checking terrain to map. One feature leads him on to the next, confirmed by his pace-counting and compass direction. However, even a good orienteerer needs to check his position accurately to within a few metres. This may happen if the map is rather old and the features – paths, plantations, etc. – have changed considerably, or if the area he is standing in is flat and featureless or on the broad slope of a large featureless hill.

In such a situation, adopt the following procedure: (1) Choose two or three landmarks in widely differing directions. In this case the church and prominent hill are obvious landmarks, with the railway bridge behind you as a third point for treble-checking (Fig. 24).

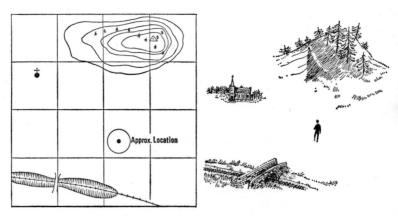

Fig. 24. Finding your location (1)

72

(*Above left*) The face of beauty and intelligence. Ulla Lundqvist, Sweden's Elite Lady Champion. (*Above right*) 'Just like Mum and Dad'. (*Below*) 'By the pond'. That moment of elation which accompanies every successful search for a control

(*Above left*) At night, run fast but tread carefully! (*Above right*) Night events bring out the best in the orienteerer. (*Below*) Two night orienteerers with 'cats eyes' race through a stream

(*Above*) A manned checkpoint in a night event. (*Below*) The bright finish beckons you from the leafy shadows

(*Left*) Halvard Nilsson's tired legs make the last sprint. (*Below left*) Pontus Carlsson, Halvard's second great danger man. (*Below right*) Bertil Norman (20) has caught and passed Sten Olaf Carlstrom in the Finland/Sweden match in 1966

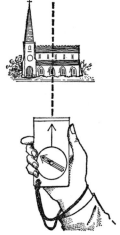

Fig. 25. Finding your location (2)

(2) Take a sight-bearing on the church with your compass. To do this hold the compass horizontal – point the direction of travel arrow at the church steeple and twist the compass housing until the compass housing arrowhead coincides with the compass needle (see Fig. 25).

(3) Now allow for Magnetic Variation by twisting the compass housing *clockwise* the appropriate number of degrees, reading the tail of the direction of travel arrow on the rim of the compass housing.

(4) Place the compass flat on the map and with the left corner by the direction of travel arrowhead on the church. Thus (A) (See Fig. 26):

Then swing the whole compass about the church until the compass housing arrowhead is parallel with the grid lines. (Obviously if you know your approximate location you will place the compass with the direction of travel across the area you believe you are in, and the 'swinging' of the compass will not involve a very great movement.) Now draw a light line along the edge of the compass passing through the church and the area of your approximate location. This is now made much more certain – you are somewhere on that line.

Now repeat the whole process, taking a sight on the prominent hill, and where the two lines intersect indicates your location to within a few yards.

A third bearing on the railway bridge, giving a third line, results in your map being marked like this (Fig. 27):

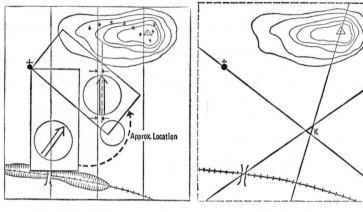

Fig. 26 Finding your location (3)

Fig. 27. Finding your location. The last step—marking the map.

You now know for certain that you are within the triangle 'K'. Lastly, you can double-check with the minor features round you and see that they agree with those featured on the map.

Now you are fully able to navigate and travel in unknown territory with complete confidence in your compass work.

You can set off in a desired direction, measuring your progress as you go along, and if you rush on with your new-found confidence and get ahead of yourself on your map, you can then check your position from landmarks in your vicinity and have no need to bother anyone else for information. Now don't give your hard-won knowledge away to those around you who are lost!

BACK-BEARING

While you are Orienteering you may need to refer to the direction you have come from. This involves what is technically called a 'back-bearing' and is merely 180° – half a revolution away from the forward bearing. There is no need for mathematics or readjustment of your compass housing because you will only have to revert to the original course-bearing before continuing. Just turn round so that the compass-needle is pointing with its South (white) end towards the compass housing arrowhead's North end (Fig. 28). This is the position you incorrectly adopt when you make a 180° error in applying your compass course. Imprint this fact on your brain! Never do it at any time except when checking a back-bearing! Finally, don't forget to spin round to the right direction once you are satisfied with the check.

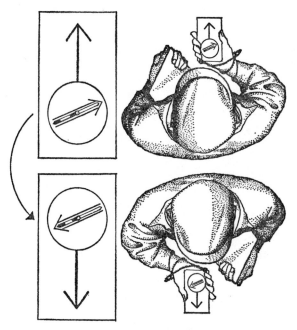

Fig. 28. Back-bearing

FOUR RIGHT-ANGLES TECHNIQUE

An Orienteering race will generally involve a detour round an obstacle in your path. It may be an unscaleable cliff, a lake or some 'out-of-bounds' property, or it may simply be terrain that is so rugged as to suggest a detour through easier country. To do this we use a four right-angles technique which is very simple and self-explanatory.

The diagram (Fig. 29) shows that it is not necessary to change the bearing on the compass. Merely run on the right angle bearing A to B by using the end edge of the compass plate for your direction of travel and revert to normal direction of travel B to C. Then use end edge once again for the leg C to D.

A confident orienteerer will take the direct course from C to E by taking a new bearing from the map. To do this he must be a good orienteerer and therefore able to say with accuracy his exact location at C on the map.

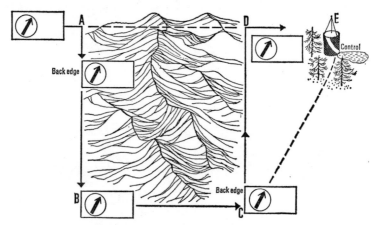

Fig. 29. Four right-angles technique

ACADEMIC POINTS

There are three Norths. That sounds Chinese but follows quite nicely on the fact that about 2500 BC it was the Chinese who took out patents on the compass. They discovered that a strip of metal ore floating on a piece of wood would take up a position pointing to the direction of the sun at midday – half-way between sunrise and sunset, or the South, as we call it. Therefore the opposite end pointed to what we call the Magnetic North. Unfortunately, simplicity is not served by the fact that the Magnetic North Pole is not at the very top of our globe – indicated by the converging grid lines of our maps and called the Geographical North Pole. The Magnetic North Pole is approximately 1,400 miles south of the Geographical. At present it is located in Northern Canada somewhere to the north of Hudson's Bay in barren, icy land quite unsuitable for Orienteering.

This is why the Magnetic Variation exists, unless you live on the Agonic Line, where there is no Magnetic Variation because you are in line with both these North Poles. The Agonic Line runs through Canada, the United States, South America, Siberia, etc. – the other half of the world (Fig. 30).

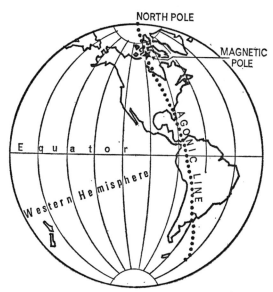

Fig. 30. The magnetic north pole and the Agonic line

In England we find that our compass points to the West of the grid North shown on our maps by about 6° to 9°. We make our Magnetic Variation adjustment as described earlier in this chapter to put things straight. The amount of Magnetic Variation obviously differs from place to place, and strangely enough this variation keeps altering about 10' to 15' (1'=1/60th of a degree) a year because the earth's Magnetic North Pole is itself drifting slowly. What then is the third North? The answer is True North, of no value to orienteerers to know, but for the record it varies by 1° E or W of grid North.

DEVELOPMENT AND TYPES OF COMPASS

Since the Chinese discovered the compass it has been developed and refined over the years. Most important to orienteerers, compass needles are now made of fine steel and balanced very finely and accurately. Not too long ago our orienteerer might have needed a very cumbersome compass to find his way, but thanks to the Swedish Kjellström family, we now use extremely light ones which fit snugly in the palm of the hand. The various types of Silva compasses are illustrated between pages 56–57.

The best compass is advised even for a novice, since it will afford him the greater satisfaction of accurate compass work. Nothing is worse than inferior equipment that produces bad results, so save up for the best – it will be the cheapest in the long run.

CHAPTER FIVE

Maps

A map is a 'picture' of the ground that enables us to find our way. The 'picture' is scaled down to a practical size that is handy and yet not too small to read the information that will tell us all about the features on the ground – hills, valleys, streams, houses and so on.

For Orienteering we use an Ordnance Survey map which shows every small detail. To suit our purposes the map has one mile of terrain shown on $2\frac{1}{2}$ in. on the map – that is, a scale of 1/25,000. An example of a section of our O/S 1/25,000 map is shown between pages 80–81.

To read and understand our map we must learn what the many signs and markings on the map represent. This map terminology is fairly straightforward and self-explanatory.

Our O/S map sheets cover an area of four square miles and cost 5/6 each, which would make an Orienteering event quite costly, especially if the course overlaps a second section of the map. Fortunately the modern invention of quick and cheap dye-line copying enables the Orienteering organiser to make inexpensive copies of the area he is using for his competition, subject to permission for reproduction from H.M. Stationery Office and on payment of a nominal royalty (see Appendix IV, page 111).

While the O/S maps are probably among the finest and most accurate in the world – and the up-to-date second series is clearer and even more accurate, with better colouring and more concise details – Orienteering in England is at a disadvantage because the black-and-white reproduction made by the copying-machine is often bad.

The O/S map is superb in four colours – blue, black, orange and grey – but after copying the general impression given is not at all clear. The blue colours for water (streams, lakes, etc.) have to be overmarked in black by the Orienteering organiser, otherwise it is not noticed at all by the copying-machine. Scandinavian orienteerers who visit England now demand the original O/S maps, preferring to use them at greater cost because they consider our black-and-white map reproductions inferior for accurate Orienteering.

Swedish competition maps are made by the Orienteering enthusiasts themselves. One map I was shown of a large forest area near Gothenburg had taken two years to make. They had examined the woods metre by metre, marking prominent features on the ground with large two-metre white crosses, making extensive notes, taking bearings and theodolite readings to ensure accurate representation of every small feature. An aerial photograph was taken on a clear day. Then, in the winter months, a 'three dimensional' visual instrument was used on two photographic copies of the terrain, and gradually the map was accurately and faithfully built up. (See map facing page 89).

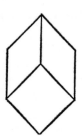

Fig. 31. This is a standard optical shape to illustrate one's inability to differentiate between inward and outward shapes. So, in a contour map without colours, how do we tell which is valley and which is hill?

The English O/S maps are fine, but the main difficulty with our black-and-white reproductions is that they are rather like the trick optical shape in Fig. 31, so far as contours are concerned – for at a glance it is not obvious which is a hilltop and which is a valley (except in very hilly country), though the colouring on the originals, as on the Swedish maps, shows instantly and unmistakably which is up and which is down. Considering that a skilled orienteerer senses his way by the contour lines rather as a blind man reads Braille, this factor is a most important one. If our Orienteering is to rely on maps for accuracy we must solve the problem of the cheap production of coloured maps, otherwise the standard of English Orienteering is going to be limited.

If you are unlucky in an event you often find that you are struggling to decipher a very bad map copy where many features are missing. Always scrutinise the map you are given and reject it if it is an inferior copy, for you are entitled to a faithful reproduction even if it is in black and white only. Another point to be cautious about is the overmarking for streams made in black ink by the organiser. Generally it cannot be strictly accurate because a zigzag method is used to mark even a straight-running stream; this helps one to pick out the water from other straight black lines. However, the source of streams or minor tributaries are quite often missed out or extended by hurrying map-markers, so do not be surprised by differences in watercourses – you are not necessarily lost!

What, then, are the points we look for on the map?

The best way to remember this is by the 'Five-D Conundrum': (1) Description, (2) Distances, (3) Details, (4) Designations, (5) Directions.

Description. This is covered by all the information round the margin of the map. At the top is the map producer, the scale and the map edition, e.g. 'Ordnance Survey scale 1/25,000 or about $2\frac{1}{2}$ in. to 1 mile – Provisional Edition'. Secondly we have the sheet number, which is shown at each corner of the map, e.g. 'Sheet TQ 14', which refers to the first figure of the two grid-lines marking the bottom left-hand corner of the sheet. (See map facing page 80). In this case they are 10 East and 40 North – thus TQ 14. At the top is marked the Magnetic Variation which applied at the time of printing, e.g. 9°30′ W. Additional information on the annual rate of change of the Magnetic Variation appears in the bottom margin of the map, together with notes on Grid North in relation to True North, viz. 'Grid N. at the centre of this sheet is 1°16′57″ E. of True North. Mag. Var. is 9°30′ W. of Grid North for June, 1956; annual change is 8′ E.' From this the organiser of the event will be able to calculate the change that has occurred to date and print the appropriate figures on his competition map reproductions for the orienteerer's benefit.

The very outer border of the map shows distance scales on the top and right-hand margin. It is in miles (0–5), with a furlong scale (0–4) at the left. Down the left side of the map the scale is in thousands of feet 0–27,000, rising up from the near bottom in hundreds 0–3,000 and downwards from the zero point. The bottom margin 0–1,000 yards in 100's and 0–9,000 yards in 1,000's. Other information written in the bottom margin of the map sheet is as follows: 'The representation on this map of a road, track or footpath is no evidence of the existence of a right of way'. This is a very important point for the orienteerer – only those with 'F.P.' printed clearly at intervals along them are public right-of-way footpaths.

The index to adjoining sheets is also there:

TQ05	TQ15	TQ25
TQ04	TQ14	TQ24
TQ03	TQ13	TQ23

This is necessary information, for one often needs the adjacent sheet or sheets for further information or for extending one's Orienteering course.

Next is the vital information: 'The grid lines on this sheet are at one-kilometre intervals'. This is the orienteerer's measure-scale – we use 100 metres calibrated in measuring and pace-counting (see Compass Chapter, 'Measuring Distance', page 67).

The information of height is below the kilometre note: 'Heights are in feet above mean sea level at Newlyn'. This is partially of interest, for it tells us how many feet rise and fall there is on the map from place to place as indicated by the figures printed on the contour lines and that each contour line is 25' above or below its neighbour – every even 100 feet at fourth contour line being marked more heavily than the intermediate heights for the 25, 50 and 75 feet contours that apply.

The other small notes cover the fact that the maps were last fully revised in 1911–34 – and partial revision made between 1938–55 having been incorporated – together with details of the Crown Copyright (for further details see Appendix).

This date is extremely important because many features may have been changed – new buildings, new roads, etc. – and even footpaths change from year to year. This will be corrected by the improved Second Series O/S maps, each sheet of which will show twice the area of these older O/S map sheets, as well as being as up to date as possible. The new maps will have green forest areas instead of the old grey, and the 'right of way' footpath is distinctively marked with green dotted lines. Also six additional symbols add to the clarity of the Second Series.

The map itself is divided by the grid-lines at 1 km. intervals to make 100 squares on the sheet (10 km. wide and long). The border of

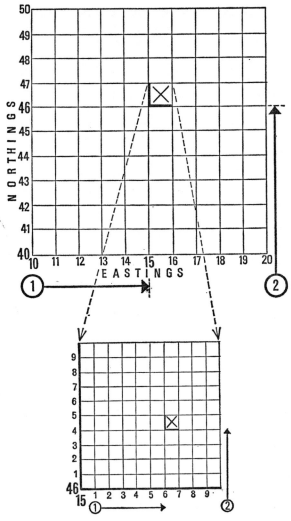

Figs. 32 & 33 (*Top*) Finding a Grid reference on an ordnance map. (*Bottom*) Obtaining a more accurate Grid reference

83

the map is marked in black and white 100-metre measures – again the orienteer's measure scale which you may copy directly on to your compass with a suitable direct marking or with a strip of adhesive paper marked with this scale.

The vertical grid lines are the 'eastings' and on this map number 10 to 20, while the horizontal ones or 'northings' are from 40 to 50. This enables handily-numbered references to be given to identify any point on the map. First, the rule for grid references is best remembered by the way we look for a certain flat-number in a large block of 100 flats made up of ten flats on ten floors. How do we do this? (1) Go along the street reading the numbers (eastings →), then (2) go up to the flat you require (northings ↑). The bottom left corner of the sheet is used as counting point for each 1 km. square; thus Square X is ... Eastings (1) – 15 ⎫
and Northings (2) – 46 ⎬ =1546 (Four Fig. Ref.)

For more accurate reference to 100 metres, imagine each square divided once again into 100 small squares.

Eastings: A *Romer* – (a handy help for the orienteer who wants to plot a reference) is made from a card with a square missing in the top right corner the same size as the 100-metre square on the map.

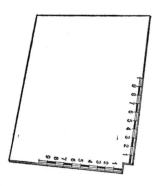

Fig. 34. A Romer

Mark 1–9 at the same 100-metre calibrations. Use to match up anywhere in this square, then read off numbers on the grid-line – Easting then Northing – exactly as with grid-lines.

Further decimilisation can be done *ad infinitum*, but a six-figure reference is accurate enough to identify a point on the map.

Having dealt with the layout and external information on the map, we can now consider how the terrain is depicted on the 'picture' of the area covered by this sheet. The forests are coloured grey with small tree symbols for coniferous or deciduous trees, and the other types of terrain speak for themselves. The Ordnance Survey produce a 'Conventional Sign Card' which gives all the necessary information.

The orange contour lines – the orienteer's 'lifelines' – tell us the shape of hills, valleys, etc. They never change as do the man-made features. Each line is 25′ above or below its neighbour (Fig. 35).

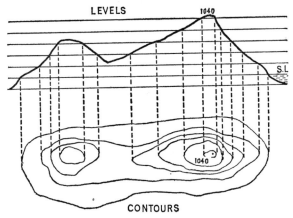

Fig. 35. How map contours work

Water is naturally blue and needs to be 'blacked in' as previously mentioned. Ponds and lakes are traced round the edge by Orienteering organisers and marked with horizontal shading.

When the Orienteering map is reproduced, subject to the conditions of copyright already mentioned, other information is added relating to the orienteer's needs before and during the competition.

The map will be headed with the name, organiser, type and date of the Orienteering event, details of the original sheet the map is reproduced from, and also the scale - although the latter is not necessary, since all Orienteering should be done on the same 1/25,000-scale maps. The 100-metre marking-scale will be shown round the whole margin of the map as it is on the original. The margin will be marked with all the grid-line numberings. The Magnetic Variation figure applying at the time of the race should be shown. No prizes are given in Orienteering for mathematical genius, so organisers should show a clean-cut figure to the nearest degree. In addition the controls will be marked on the map, as indicated under 'course-setting' for major events. For minor events, the competitors copy control-points on to their maps themselves.

Lastly, each map must bear the acknowledgement relating to the copyright and the permission of the appropriate authorities (for details see Appendix IV). 'Reproduced from the Ordnance Survey Map with the sanction of the Controller of H.M. Stationery Office. Crown Copyright reserved.'

CHAPTER SIX

Orienteering Equipment and Training

ORIENTEERING EQUIPMENT

The competitor must be properly clad for running over rough terrain. A pair of strong studded or grip shoes worn with socks and long lightweight slacks usually of nylon – or alternatively, long stockings to protect the foreleg and a pair of rugby-style shorts – will suit the purpose admirably. For the 'wayfarers' ordinary walking shoes or boots will do the job together with a pair of old slacks. Depending on the weather it is possible to wear a short-sleeved singlet or a long-sleeved football jersey.

The Elite orienteerer uses a nylon top which matches the nylon slacks. These special suits are fine for all weathers and have pockets on the chest and the right foreleg. They come in very handy for odd pieces of equipment one carries. Headwear is also necessary for those who penetrate woods. A peaked cap is a good safety measure to protect the eyes from being scratched by tree branches or brambles. Finally the indispensable items for the orienteerer are his compass, map-case and red marker-pen. The pen must be one with non-running ink so that the course marked on the map does not disappear in wet conditions. For the convenience of the orienteerer it is handy to have a roll of thin adhesive tape that will not fail when immersed in water. This tape is used to fix the stamp card on to the back of the map-case.

Selecting a compass can be an interesting moment and those described between pages 56–57 are available to all orienteerers.

It is worth while to invest in the best model whether you wish to be a champion orienteerer or a 'wayfarer'.

Officials will need the same equipment as competitors – for as explained in the course-setting 'Bible' of SOFT reproduced on pages 97–106 – the official must keep up to date by competing in Orienteering.

For the purposes of course-setting the official will need additional equipment which can be made or purchased.

A set of marker-flags can be made according to the descriptions on page 54. A complete set numbers something between twenty and thirty. Each flag must bear a letter or number and it is best to attach to each flag a self-inking stamp bearing this key.

For start-and-finish streamers crêpe paper can be bought and cut into strips. A few lengths of rope and steel posts can be borrowed.

Boards are needed for attaching master maps (20). Hardboard can be used for this purpose – cut into pieces about 1' to 2' square.

Polythene bags or sheeting are needed for protecting the master maps.

A large stopwatch or chronometer is recommended in addition to officials' wrist watches all of which should be synchronised well before the start.

Lastly, warm, waterproof clothing is a 'must' for officials who spend hours in doing their skilled work and awaiting the competitors' return.

TRAINING FOR ORIENTEERING

Physical training for Orienteering is not difficult. All that is necessary is to make a short run up to twenty or thirty minutes two or three times in the week and to race on Sundays.

It is far better to be fresh for Orienteering, as it is for athletics, so do not overdo the exercise. Good fitness results from consistent activity over a long period, not from feverish and exhausting programmes of racing oneself to death. So avoid all 'Interval' training or other kinds of exhaustive exercise. Wait until the competition to run hard. You will achieve your best results in Orienteering through freshness, and thus you will enjoy the sport and progress from strength to strength in a physical sense.

For Orienteering training take an O/S 25,000 map sheet of the

Sketch map, based on the master map for the 1966 Euro Meeting at Bohuslän, north of Gothenburg, showing method of numbering control points and joining them with straight red lines to clarify the control order in point events.

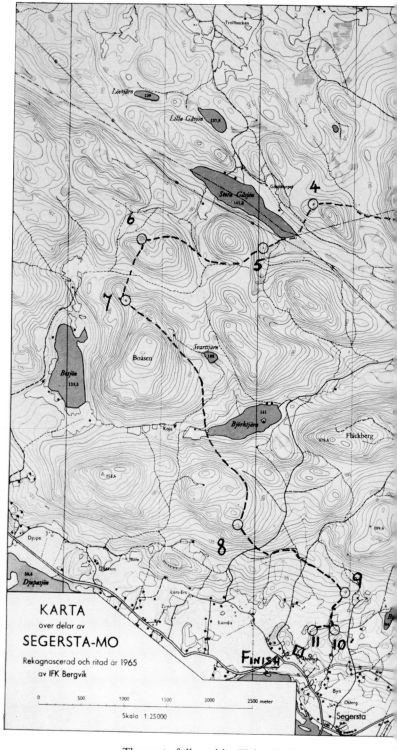

The route followed by Halvard Nilsson when winning

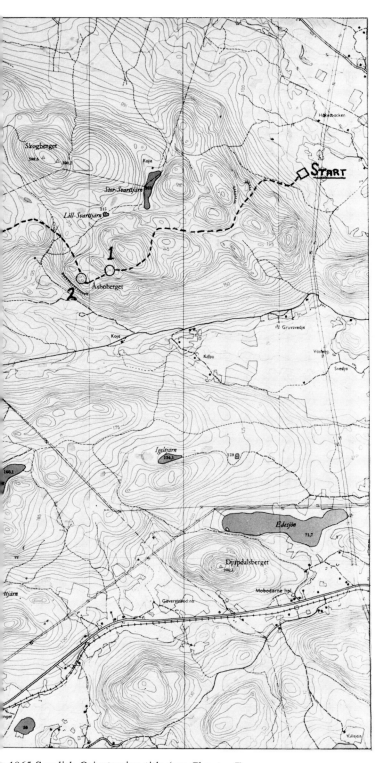

1965 Swedish Orienteering title (see Chapter 7)

A section of a Swedish orienteering map, accurately and faithfully built up as described in the text

area you may use, together with your full running and Orienteering kit as outlined in the equipment section. Select features on the map and choose your route. Practise your compass drills for finding direction of travel; measure the distances you will run and practise step-counting. Alternatively, try finding your way by recognising features only, without compass and distance drills. Thirdly, you may try memorising your route choice and run without further reference to your map or compass.

When progressing through the terrain always take the easiest way and run to the nearest 'catching' feature to the control point you have selected. Then stop, carefully take a bearing to the control and measure the distance, taking note of the features *en route*, and deliberately and meticulously go the last few metres to the feature. It takes great self-control to switch from running hard for several hundred metres to steady, restrained progress during the last metres. Slow but sure is the watchword because it is in the final approach to the control that errors must be eliminated.

Only through this continual practice 'in the field', in the true conditions of Orienteering and with actual competitions providing the additional tension which destroys many otherwise good competitors, will you develop your Orienteering skills.

Mental training may be done any evening by use of an Orienteering map. Choose a feature on the map and look for a second feature some 400–600 metres or even 2 km. away. Study the choice of routes and decide in a few seconds which way you would go in practice. Memorise the route and try to picture it without the map. Remember the curved path – the stream – the bridge – the path junction – the hill and the marsh and the valley. This is how the trained orienteer sharpens his wits. The great runners in Sweden think nothing of reading the map in this fashion for an hour every evening before turning out the light at bedtime.

At the start of an event study the map from the moment you receive it. Study it as you race – this I do at every available stride, often looking at the map too much and falling in difficult ground as a result. I have a picture of my map imprinted on my brain after a few minutes and am able to correlate my position on the ground with it as I progress. I study the close vicinity on the map and the terrain surrounding me, but also the general picture of the surrounding square mile of territory on the map. I am ready to welcome the next feature over the hill or round the corner, and so can race at break-neck speed across the countryside – accurately, but easing up to double-check the last metres to the control flag. On approaching the control you should study the route out from the control, because you should not stop at a control flag more than a couple of seconds, otherwise you may give its position away to other competitors. As I reach the control I have already imprinted the next stages of the course on to my brain.

CHAPTER SEVEN

A Champion's Route

My second Swedish Orienteering title, 1965
by Halvard Nilsson (Skellefteå Club)

Properly speaking, it is quite impossible to describe objectively what one feels when achieving a great personal success in sport, particularly during the competition itself. The feelings and experiences of the winner are, in fact, little different from those of the other competitors, most of whom may never be granted 100% success in a competition or be the lucky person Fate decides shall come at the top of the results list – the position every orienteer struggles passionately to attain. Very seldom, if ever, have a competitor's feelings been adequately expressed in words, but here goes!

The day of the 1965 Swedish Orienteering Championship apparently dawned like nearly all the competition days I have experienced – although, in retrospect, I have to admit it seems to have been just that little bit different. Even the weather appeared a little more beautiful, the sky brighter and all the colours more intense than they normally are.

We train and struggle for hundreds – no, thousands – of hours in all weathers and on dark winter evenings in order to harden our bodies so that they will be able to cope physically with the heavy exertions they will have to bear for 10 miles during a championship competition. Our mental and psychological faculties will also probably be trained just as highly. In my opinion, orienteering is, first of all, a competition of self control and power of concentration. How many times have I stood on the starting-line, completely trained, and with a 'motor' that should have brought victory provided no mistakes were made – and yet the race has ended in great disappointment because my concentration failed at the critical moment. Often it has been just a trifling matter that has upset my concentration: I have perhaps run a few metres too much to one side of a copse, or have been careless for a second just when I reached a key feature.

After many years, the necessary care and attention have, however, become ingrained. Through the knowledge of being physically well-trained, self-confidence has developed and created the pre-requisites for that calm concentration which is absolutely necessary for success in Orienteering. But achieving this has cost me, and many other Swedish orienteers, many disappointments, and ten, maybe fifteen, years to reach such a standard of skill. Things are, however, a little easier now, thanks to the very good maps made by the orienteerers themselves in almost every country belonging to the Orienteering family.

On this special day in 1965, I knew I had a good chance, but I also knew there would be very stiff competition. The terrain had a great rise and fall across the whole of the map (see page 88–89) but as you can see, it was not particularly undulating or steeply inclined, so I would be able to run all the way up and down the hills. Although the competition was being held 400 miles from my home, the terrain was rather like the district where I lived, and that would suit me excellently. Also, sunshine has always delighted me, and I have been most successful when the sun has been out and the weather warm.

I decided to accelerate to my highest speed right from the start because, judging from the course profile, the most difficult stretch would be at the beginning, and there would be little point in conserving energy for the later stages. Going downhill you can run even when you are very tired.

As you can see from my marked route on the map between pages 88–89, the course to the first control (1) was terrible. I preferred going almost straight over the last hill as the routes around it seemed to me to be too long. In Orienteering you always have to choose – to compare advantages and disadvantages. But most important of all is that you must never hesitate, but carry through the decision you have made with determination. The small marsh was situated rather openly and was not difficult to find. With regard to the second control (2), I chose to go up on the hill to the left and then follow it to the depression. I would not risk coming to the right side of the control, in case I went too far to the right. This control was radio-controlled, and of course I was encouraged to notice that I had the best time at that moment. Such information could, however, be dangerous in Orienteering. You must not lose control of your nerves, be too eager, or too encouraged. Your time is to be measured at the finish – and for me that was a long way off.

On the way to the third control (3) there was a trap. Everybody who tried to go straight to the control – and most of the competitors did – made an enormous height-loss and had a very heavy slope to contend with on the opposite side of the creek. As you can see from the map, I went around to the right. That choice of route was one of the fundamental reasons for my eventual success, for as a result I opened up a lead of 2 minutes. Fortunately, I knew nothing of this, at least with any certainty, but I did have a feeling that I was doing very well. Later, at the finish, I heard that the two competitors I feared most, Pontus Carlsson and Bertil Norman, were 2 and 3 minutes respectively behind me at this stage.

To reach the next control (4), I just had to go straight on, while the fifth one (5), the charcoal kiln, presented no problems. However, this charcoal kiln could have been dangerous, and I was lucky to have been careful over the last few metres from the finish of the marsh. Bertil Norman lost 3 minutes here in the thick copse that has grown up on ground well fertilised by the charcoal ashes!

On my way to the sixth control (6) – situated at the foot of a hill, it was also a radio and refreshment control – I suppose I must have made an unnecessary detour to the right. Some runners had a time one minute better than me between the fifth and sixth controls. However, by this time, I had a lead of 7 minutes. I did not know this then, but did feel I was beginning to get the race sewn up. However, if somebody had told me that after 6 miles I had a lead of 7 minutes – that is, more than one minute per mile – I would have bet 1,000 kronor that either he was a liar or the time-keeper's watch was wrong! In fact, the time was right, 59 minutes!

The report of my time to control point six was sent directly by radio to the finish, and everybody there could check it. Besides, the report was the last one from that particular control. Maybe the transmitter was shocked by the time it had to pass on! Later, there was some newspaper talk of a world orienteering record for six miles. I just do not know anything about that as – fortunately – we cannot possibly establish such records in orienteering. However, everything had been unusually perfect on this lovely day – and maybe there are one or two persons, here and there, who regard themselves secretly as world champions in Orienteering for a certain part of a certain race and over suitably chosen distances! Isn't that rather wonderful? Psychologically, it certainly was!

Then I was on the way 'home'. The seventh control (7), a boundary cairn, was easy to find on the ridge-back. Then followed a long leg to the next control (8), which seemed to be difficult. Controls out on large slopes are always difficult, especially if the control point is in a depression as this one was. However, when a control is difficult, it need not be dangerously so provided **you** can see from the map that it *is* difficult. It is much more troublesome when you are going to a control that *seems* to be easy but in reality is difficult. So you had better regard all controls as difficult!

To reach the eighth control, I could go straight over the high hill, and follow the path up to the small cabin on the next hill, or I could choose to go around the first hill – to the left or to the right – and eventually go around the next hill too. As you can see, I chose to go around it to the left. Going up the last hills from the lake, my legs said 'no', and I had to tell them again and again that there was just a little bit uphill left, and then downhill all the way to the finish.

From the eighth control to the ninth (9), there was need for 'safety first'. By now, I was sure that if I didn't get a leg or an ankle broken, or something else equally crippling, I really could win the race. The boulder at the ninth control was rather difficult to find, and I was a little lucky to meet a couple of runners just coming from it! The last two controls (10 and 11) were merely to collect the runners before the finish, so were negotiated quickly.

I have many times wondered how tired you have to be not to be carried along on wings when you have spotted the finishing flag, heard the shouts of the people waiting there, and the metallic sound of the loud-speaker – or maybe not hearing them but rather sensing their nearness. You are then suddenly able to give 200% of yourself.

After I had finished, there followed an hour of hope and desperation, self-criticism and reproaches, as I waited for the late-starters to arrive at the finish. In my imagination I was especially afraid of Bertil Norman. About his progress we had learnt nothing since the wireless transmitter collapsed with electronic heart failure when I passed control six. However, the hour ticked slowly by, Bertil arrived with the third best time, I made the expected TV speech, and it was time to start a very pleasant journey home, bringing with me, among other prizes, a fully automatic wrist-watch as a memento of my second Swedish Championship – I won my first in 1956. In Sweden for many years we have had a familiar saying: 'They never come back.' That is, nobody could win the Swedish Championship more than once. However, three of us have now managed to win it twice. The other two are Anders Morelius and Pontus Carlsson.

To win the Swedish Championship is the dream of every Swedish orienteerer. I suppose the reason is the very large number of superb orienteerers in Sweden. At every Swedish Championship only about 100 of the best ones are chosen to start, and I can assure you that the struggle for a place in the starting-list is always very keen.

However, the most wonderful experience of all for me was when I arrived home at my club, and found that my friends, although it was midnight, had arranged a pathway of flaming torches to greet me, followed by a heart-warming celebration.

I am indeed very happy to have been a Swedish champion in Orienteering.

HALVARD NILSSON

SWEDISH ORIENTEERING CHAMPIONSHIPS 1965

ORGANISERS: IFK Bergvik.
COURSE-SETTER: Carl-Erik Jonsson and Helge Wiklund.
MAP SCALE: 1 : 25,000.
COURSE DISTANCE: 13.7 km.
START. South-east end of the marsh.
CONTROL 1. In the marsh.
CONTROL 2. The west end of the depression.
CONTROL 3. In the depression.
CONTROL 4. The west side of the boulder.
CONTROL 5. The charcoal-burning ground.
CONTROL 6. The south-east foot of the hill.
CONTROL 7. The boundary cairn.
CONTROL 8. High in the re-entrant.

CONTROL 9. The south side of the double boulder.
CONTROL 10. The charcoal-burning ground.
CONTROL 11. The edge of the field.
Follow streamers 250 metres to the finish.

RESULTS:

	1	2	3	4	5	6	7	8	9	Finish	Total Time
1. Halvard Nilsson, Skellefteå	20	3	13	10	5	8	4	26	9	3.15	1.41.15
2. Anders Morelius	21	3	15	11	5	10	5	23	9	2.47	1.44.47
3. Bertil Norman	20	3	17	11	8	7	4	25	10	3.00	1.48.00
4. Per Olof Skogum	26	3	15	10	5	8	5	25	9	3.07	1.49.07
5. Sven-Olof Asberg	22	3	13	11	9	8	5	27	10	2.59	1.50.59
Göran Öhlund	22	3	15	12	6	9	5	25	10	3.59	1.50.59
7. Pontus Carlsson	22	3	13	10	5	9	4	34	8	3.05	1.51.05
8. Lars Roos	23	3	15	11	7	6	5	27	11	3.43	1.51.43
9. Ingemar Hedén	23	3	14	11	7	13	4	25	9	3.05	1.52.05
10. Olle Hermansson	22	3	15	11	9	10	4	27	9	3.14	1.53.14
11. Sture Björk	23	3	15	13	6	10	5	26	9	3.25	1.53.25
12. Östen Sahr	26	3	15	10	7	10	5	25	9	3.36	1.53.46

The results show how close the competition in Sweden is. As Halvard Nilsson says – all are champions who make the Swedish Championship races!

CHAPTER EIGHT

The Course-Setter's Handbook

The Rules for setting orienteering courses, as worked out at the Scandinavian Course-Setters' Conference, in Stockholm, 3rd and 4th December, 1966
Reproduced by kind permission of SOFT (Swedish Orienteering Förbund)

The aim for the course-setter is to make a competition which gives a fair result based upon the competitors' Orienteering ability. Therefore every course-setter has two main aims:

A. To organise a fair and sporting race.

B. To ensure that the individual character of the Orienteering-running is maintained.

A. SPORTING QUALITIES

The course-setter must strive to produce in every detail a course which will make equal demands upon the Orienteering ability of each and every competitor. Chance must play no part in the result of the competition.

The following main points are responsible for depriving competitions of their fair nature and so deprive events of their sporting quality.

1. THE MAP. The map must be a mirror of the actual terrain to which it refers. Since the runners' progress across the terrain relies entirely upon their map-reading and consequently, their choice of route depends upon the accuracy of the map, the map's 'mirroring' the terrain, then it follows that the fairness of the event depends

upon the quality of the map. Without a good map it is not possible to set a fair competition in which all competitors will have an equal chance to win, because any inaccuracy may impede one runner who happens to choose his route passing through areas not correctly charted, whereas another competitor, having chosen a different route across an accurately charted area on the map, will have an unfair advantage.

Therefore an accurate map is the first consideration in setting a fair course for all competitors.

2. THE CONTROLS

(a) *Siting:* First, the control point must be accurately sited at the exact location on the terrain as indicated by the map.

(b) *Control Vicinity:* Second, the terrain in the close vicinity of the control point must be exactly as shown on the map.

(c) *Control Approaches:* The main features on the approaches to the control which the competitors will be likely to use as 'stepping stones' to start their final run to the control – all these features must be accurate in their distance and direction from the control point.

(d) *Control Difficulty:* The control difficulty must be selected to match the standard of the competition.

(e) *Control Definition:* The actual control point must be as described in the control definition.

3. PLACING THE FLAG. The flag must mark the exact point of the control as marked on the map at the very centre point of the control circle which is used to indicate the control point on the map.

The positioning of the flag with regard to its height and visibility to the incoming runners must be varied to suit the differing conditions that apply to each control.

For example, if one may run directly to a control by use of the map only, then the flag may be placed so low that it is not visible to the competitor until he has reached the control point.

On the other hand, if one must run on a compass bearing to a small feature on the terrain which skill will not entail map reading at all, then the flag must be placed at such a height relative to the distance covered on the compass bearing – i.e. a short distance would warrant the low placing of the flag or a long distance justifies a high placing of the flag. This particular rule will also be modified in accordance with the quality of the 'catching' front of the control point. For example, if the control point is sited on a strong feature then the flag will be placed lower than if the feature is a very minor one.

The flag must be placed in such a way as to avoid open terrain with the competitors who have found the control giving its position away to other competitors who have not yet found the flag.

4. THE ROUTE CHOICES. A course which offers the choice of several alternative routes between control points will spread the competitors throughout the terrain and so ensure that individuals must rely on their own Orienteering skills. This contributes towards a fairer competition.

The competitors' freedom of choice of route – the greatest quality of the sport of Orienteering – must in no circumstances result in an element of good or bad luck having a decisive influence on the result. Any element of chance must be eliminated.

Choosing the best route must never involve such a terribly complicated choice between the alternative routes available which cannot be reasoned out by a clever orienteerer.

Every choice of route which the map indicates as feasible must also be feasible in practice over the terrain.

A chosen route must not in practice turn out to be easier and faster than indicated by the map picture. For example, by way of a path which is not shown on the map but is now on the terrain.

Alternatively a chosen route must not be harder in practice than indicated by the map picture. For example, a flooded area or difficult rocks not shown on the map.

The choice of route must not allow any element of luck to enter into the result of the Orienteering race.

5. THE COURSE LAYOUT. Each leg of the course must be carefully planned and adjusted relative to the other legs so that the course as a whole will not allow luck to enter into the running of the competition.

Controls must be so situated as to eliminate the situation of runners going to a control being led in to the control flag by those runners who have found the flag and are leaving the control point. This does occur when 'dog-legs' exist on a course, i.e. when the incoming and outgoing routes are in an acute angle to each other so offering a common route to and from a control.

When a course shows legs which cross each other, or when the course is such that the competitors may, by different route choices, cause the same terrain to be crossed, then when these two possibilities exist on a course the course must be shown to all competitors before the start to enable all to make their own route choices in advance of the competition start.

B. THE INDIVIDUALITY OF THE ORIENTEERING RUNNING

Equally important to make a Sporting competition the course-setter's second aim is to set a course which poses problems to the runners which will guarantee the individuality of the Orienteering running.

ORIENTEERING AND RUNNING

The individual nature of the Orienteering skill and that of the running is to be equally apportioned and both must exist throughout the competition. If either is not an element of each and every part of the race then the course-setter has not catered for the individuality of the sport.

To satisfy the need for good running is the easiest task for the course-setter. Although competitors need to stop to read the map – this does not eliminate testing their endurance because the distance of the competition has to be covered by each individual on his own.

The course-setter must balance the running with a demand for an equal amount of Orienteering skill from each individual on every leg of the course and so preserve the individuality of the Orienteering and running.

Any section of the course which does not demand Orienteering skills equally with running ability means a failure on the part of the course-setter. At all times a good course throws a simultaneous demand upon the individual's Orienteering skill and his running ability.

Therefore the most important points for guaranteeing the individuality of the Orienteering and Running are as follows:

1. CHOICE OF TERRAIN. The competition area will be a decisive factor for the course-setter.

Featureless terrain is bad. Hilly, variable and many featured terrain is the ideal to be sought after because it will offer the course-setter chances to pose difficult problems necessitating careful Orienteering.

However, terrain with many catching features such as roads, railways, large streams or rivers, many buildings or open terrain and cultivated ground are to be avoided since the Orienteering problems will not be demanding.

Also, terrain with large cliffs or extremely difficult going underfoot by way of many boulders should also be avoided. The terrain must, on the whole, be practical for hard running.

Lastly, after the course-setter has chosen his area then he must set the course in such a way as to utilise the best Orienteering terrain and avoid the worst. Where the terrain is best suited to Orienteering – there the course must be drawn.

2. MAP-READING. The map-reading in Orienteering demands mental concentration so this is a most important factor to be taken into account by the course-setter. Every control and every leg of the course must be carefully planned so that the competitor is required to employ map-reading skills as much as possible. Anything that will exclude or simplify the map-reading for the competitor should be excluded from the competition. Therefore the course-setter will choose the course in such a way as to avoid all the large and easily recognised features (fields, roads, lakes, etc.). If controls are placed beyond such major 'catching' features then the skills of Orienteering will not be present – only the running without thinking will remain. Each section of the course which has running only to major features is a section in which the course maker has lost an equal distance in map-reading.

The course-setter, for the longer major legs of the course, must make use of the best terrain which is most detailed on the map so demanding careful map-reading skill.

The longer the distance is from the last 'attack' point (a definitely recognisable feature), to the control point through difficult terrain, the greater is the demand for care and attention in map-reading.

3. THE ROUTE CHOICE. Route choice is a most important and valuable factor in making a good Orienteering traverse of difficult terrain and route choosing considerably increases the mental problems.

Course setters must, therefore, devote great attention to make their choice of course offer the competitors as many route alternatives as possible between the control points.

Any choice of route which will eliminate all mental effort must be avoided completely and such a choice of route should not exist to afford success to the very good runner who could employ a minimum of mental effort for his success.

Above all, the course-setter must attempt to ensure that the quickest route between the controls will also demand the greatest mental effort in map-reading and Orienteering skills.

The course-setter seeks to make a selection of controls which will necessitate more calculation and mental effort from the competitor. The mental effort must not be restricted to the problem of choosing the route between the controls – but also involve balancing out the pros and cons of distance versus difficulty. The route choice is meant to increase not decrease the Orienteering problems.

4. THE FUNCTION OF THE CONTROL. Each control must fulfil a rôle. There must be an idea or an intention behind every control choice.

The first function the control must fulfil is to produce a leg of a good long stretch, filled with the need for map reading, route choosing and running – in fact, involving the use of as many Orienteering skills as possible.

Secondly, a control can be used to complete only a short distance in order to give a better starting place for the next longer leg of the course in such a way as to avoid what would otherwise be a 'dog-leg' and its pitfalls already related.

Each control which serves a special purpose as above is valuable – but every control without special function is a mistake of the course-setter – and is one extra, unnecessary control.

5. THE CHOICE OF THE CONTROL POINT. The course-setter will attempt to place the control where he needs it most – but will adapt the exact location to suit the map and the terrain conditions.

The control point must not be so large and obvious that it reduces the demand made upon the competitors' Orienteering skills and not necessitate complete concentration by the competitor over the last few metres to the control. Small and difficult 'catching' points should be sought out, so demanding more map reading, concentration and skilful Orienteering the closer the competitor comes to the control.

Thus the course-setter will strive to set difficult problems to the competitor by the difficult long stretch between the control points and the difficulties presented in the locality of the control.

THE START AND THE FINISH OF THE COURSE

The start and finish of the course are important both from the point of view of providing a fair and sporting race and for ensuring the individuality of the Orienteering.

THE START. The start must be placed in such a way as to offer first-class Orienteering right from the start. In order that the runners will start in good Orienteering terrain the distance from the changing and pre-start area, marked by paper streamers, is allowed to be long. It is better for the competitors to go one kilometre longer to the time start than to run the first kilometre in unsuitable terrain.

The start must be hidden from those runners who have not started. The start place must be accurately shown on the map and correctly sited on the ground.

THE FINISH. The finish demands the greatest care and attention. In order that finish times may be recorded to the exact second the referees and time keepers must have an unobstructed view of the finish which should be a one direction funnel and arranged in such a way that all the competitors must come from the same direction.

In order that the finish does not deprive the race of too much time and distance which should be taken up with the competitors concentrating on their Orienteering and running skills, the finish distance from the last control should be short. The last control is, therefore, placed very near to the finish and the pure running sprint finish over the line can be short and not too difficult from a physical point of view.

The finish area itself must be open and 'catching' for the competitors and affording a good view for the spectators to cheer on the last efforts of the competitors as they fight with each other for vital seconds.

DISTANCES FOR PAPER STREAMERS. At the start and finish of the course the course-setter is usually obliged to make use of paper streamers.

Running along the streamer trail is rather irrelevant to the real Orienteering so it is wise to keep the length of streamer trails as short as possible.

If the terrain will only allow a run free from Orienteering to the finish funnel then the course-maker must arrange a streamer trail from the last control to the finish. This streamer trail should not be laid in such a way as to offer a lucky chance to a competitor as a 'catching' line. As an alternative the streamer trail may be marked on the map so that all competitors know of the location of the streamers, so eliminating the element of chance.

Finally, make every streamer trail as short as possible but do not forget that every metre not concerned with Orienteering skills is of no value to the Competition.

c. THE COURSE FOR NIGHT EVENTS

The Orienteering technique for night events is not quite the same as that required for day events. Therefore the construction of the course for a night event will in several important aspects demand a different technique from that used for day events.

1. THE 'PLAN' PICTURE. Night Orienteering in very thick forest means that the skills of compass reading and distance measuring are mainly employed in these events, but in order that map reading can also be involved to a reasonable degree an area must be used in which many detailed features exist which will oblige the use of map-reading skill. Features such as roads, paths, fields and buildings are necessary in a night event area to bring in more mental problems for the orienteerer to solve.

Night Orienteering is mostly done from the 'Plan' picture that the map presents. Therefore the course-setter must choose terrain which is rich in detailed features. This is especially important when the night event is held in a forest.

Caution should be exercised that night events will not encroach upon 'out-of-bounds' areas – such as cultivated ground and gardens etc., which would provide the temptation for breaking the rules and make the competition unfair because of the element of luck coming into the race.

2. RALLYING – CATCHING POINTS. Normally night Orienteering will not be more hazardous and difficult than events held in the daytime. In order to achieve this it is important that the night event controls are placed in the correct terrain.

The night control must always have safety 'catching' points at the right distance beyond the control where the competitor, after a possible mistake, can re-orientate himself and retrace his steps back to the control vicinity in a reasonable time.

3. THE NIGHT CONTROL. The character of the control is especially important in night Orienteering.

The controls must be chosen so that competitors are not attracted by the torchlight of other competitors at a distance – so losing Orienteering moments.

On the hill, on the summit and other such controls visible from a distance are unsuitable for night events. Therefore the majority of night controls should be at points on the terrain which will hide the light. For example in the gulley, in the re-entrant, in the ravine, etc.

When a night control is marked with a flag rather than a lamp it should be located accurately at a point which can be reached by map-reading, taking the competitor right to the flag.

Thus unsuitable night controls would be those points which are on diffuse features without sharpness: for example – the edge of the marsh, the re-entrant, the foot of the hill, etc. On the other hand suitable controls would be those with 'sharpness' – the corner of the field, the bend of the stream, the path junction etc., where the flag can be accurately and precisely placed.

NB If only a flag (not a light) is used for control points the competitors must be informed that this is so before the start of the competition.

4. ROUTE CHOICE. Route choice is an important factor in night course, where the competitor forsakes compass-running to follow faster and more easily negotiated routes. This he does in a rather different way to normal day events.

Because the night orienteerer cannot run carelessly and without map-reading in the hope of 'catching' features to find his location quickly, he must know at all times his exact location and not lose contact with the map picture.

Therefore, the night event course-setter can offer long legs with many alternative routes – in a way which may be quite different to the day course possibilities. A long leg which traverses roads, fields, paths and a number of other catching-points need not mean that map-reading is dispensed with but rather that the map-reading problems are increased.

Problems of route choice which are too complicated and involve too many kilometres can bring in an element of chance and spoil the event, as is possible in a day event as well.

The route choice must not be a puzzle the right solution of which is the crucial factor in the result of the competition – rather than the main Orienteering skills being the deciding element.

SUMMING UP

The theoretical rules of course-setting must direct the course in such a way as to guarantee the individual quality of the Orienteering-running and produce a fair and sporting event. This is a timeless aim which makes our sport today and in the future.

In order that the course-setter may cleverly put into practice the theory of course-setting he must be an enthusiast. He must be keenly aware of the finer points of Orienteering, maps and map-reading, competition rules, competition organisation and must compete himself, following the continual development of the sport. Competing is the best way for a course-setter to have his hand on the very pulse of the sport of Orienteering.

THE COURSE CONTROL

Besides creating the problems of the controls the course-setter pays attention to the quality and safety of the competition and therefore he must use great care in his work.

The course controls must be set out well in advance of the competition time so that the course-setter may also be responsible for the following principal functions:

1. Ensure that the master maps and courses are completed in good time.

2. Be available to answer queries on the course arrangements and course distances.

3. Check that the start, the controls and the finish are in order and correct according to all the conditions set out in these rules.

All the officials assisting in the course-making and organisation must also know the competition rules.

Stockholm, 3rd-4th December, 1966.
Hans Andersen and Helmuth Olsen—Denmark.
Osmo Niemelä and Heikki Wollsten—Finland.
Alf Stefferud and Per Wang—Norway.
Folke Franzon and Elof Jägerström—Sweden.

Orienteering Associations

BRITISH ORIENTEERING FEDERATION (see Appendix V).

For all information regarding Orienteering in Great Britain, including details of the Regional Associations listed below, please contact:

> Mrs. Patricia Norris,
> B.O.F. National Office,
> 11 Balmoral Crescent,
> West Molesey,
> Surrey.

(Tel: 01–979 6345)

The Regional Associations:

THE NORTHERN ORIENTEERING ASSOCIATION (covers Lancashire, Cheshire, Cumberland, Westmorland and Yorkshire).

THE WEST MIDLANDS ORIENTEERING ASSOCIATION (covers Staffordshire, Shropshire, Worcestershire, Warwickshire and Herefordshire).

THE NORTH MIDLANDS ORIENTEERING ASSOCIATION (covers Derbyshire, Nottinghamshire, Lincolnshire, Leicestershire and Northampton-shire).

THE SOUTH WEST ORIENTEERING ASSOCIATION (covers Gloucestershire, Wiltshire, Somerset, Dorset, Devon and Cornwall).

THE SOUTHERN ORIENTEERING ASSOCIATION (covers Surrey, London, Sussex, Kent, Essex, Hertfordshire, Hampshire and Middlesex).

THE SCOTTISH ORIENTEERING ASSOCIATION.

APPENDIX II

The Country Code

Every competitor shall show consideration toward wild life and vegetation. It is forbidden to set foot on newly-sown ground, on growing crops or any area where the farmer has made efforts to keep animals away. Great care should be taken when crossing fences or ditches. Gates should be left as you find them.

All obvious private property is out of bounds.

APPENDIX III

Duke of Edinburgh's Award Scheme

FITNESS SECTION: ORIENTEERING

This activity may be offered as part of the Fitness Section at Silver and Gold Stages of the Scheme. The candidates will be judged by the Assessors of the English Orienteering Association, in accordance with the following conditions:

1. *Practical Tests*

Candidates should in the period that they are engaged in the Award Scheme achieve the following standard in practical Orienteering. They must achieve this standard in at least two open races approved by the English Orienteering Association.

Note. Most of the competitions that are indicated on the Regional and National Fixture Lists will be acceptable; however, Score Events will not be counted, neither will events be considered where boys enter and compete in pairs. This will probably bar night events for boys competing in Junior Races.

SILVER AWARD. (a) For boys under 16 – to achieve a time which is better than the average of the first three boys home plus fifty per cent of this time in a Junior (over 15 and under 18 on the day of competition) cross-country Orienteering competition. E.g.:

1st Jones	50 min. 02 sec.
2nd Brian	54 min. 10 sec.
3rd Kent	60 min. 04 sec.

$$\text{Average} = \frac{164 \text{ min. } 16 \text{ sec.}}{3} = 54 \text{ min. } 45 \text{ sec.}$$

109

54 min. 45 sec.
$+$ 27 min. 22 sec.

Award Pass Time= 82 min. 07 sec.

(b) For boys over 18 – to achieve a time which is better than the average of the first three boys plus seventy-five per cent of this time in an Intermediate (over 18 and under 21 on the day of competition) cross-country Orienteering event.

GOLD AWARD. Boys must achieve a time which is better than the average of the first three boys plus fifty per cent of this time in an Intermediate cross-country Orienteering competition.

2. *Theory Test*

Examiners appointed by the English Orienteering Association will conduct an oral test for those candidates who have successfully completed the Practical Test. Where possible this test will be held in conjunction with an Orienteering event.

The questions asked in the test will relate to the following aspects of Orienteering:

(a) Types of Event – point, score, line, night, etc., the general organisation of these events, team scoring, relay work.

(b) The Rules of the Competition.

(c) Control Terminology and definition of features.

(d) Techniques and skills – choice of routes, use of guide-lines, aiming-off, collecting-features, step-counting, height v. distance, rough v. smooth, etc.

(e) Training – map and compass techniques, physical fitness.

(f) Course-setting – suitable country, control-siting, selecting problems, positioning, the markers, etc.

(g) Country Code, Orienteering code of conduct and safety.

(h) Equipment.

(i) History and present state of the sport in this country.

Candidates will be expected to be reasonably knowledgeable about all the above aspects of the sport, and to be able to answer straightforward questions, not only about competing, but also about the organisation of an event.

All communications on this aspect of the Duke of Edinburgh's Scheme should be addressed to the appropriate Regional Secretary. (See Appendix I).

Map Reproduction
(N.B. All prices quoted subject to change.)

1. Rank Xerox (Electrostatic process).
   Cost per 100 copies: £3 15s. 0d.
   (At this price copies will be produced by return post or while you wait).
   London office: Remax House,
   31/32 Alfred Place,
   Store Street,
   London, W.C.1.
   Telephone: LANgham 9561 and MUSeum 4935.
   Other service facilities in Birmingham, Manchester, Newcastle-on-Tyne and Glasgow.
2. Rank (Offset plate process).
   Cost of plate: 12s., then 13s. per 100 copies.
   (Several days' notice is needed for this work to be done).
   Addresses as above.
3. The Universal Drawing Office (Group of Companies).
   (Dyeline prints process).
   Cost of photograph: 15s. 9d., then 6d. per copy.
   Universal Drawing Office, Ltd.,
   28 North Audley Street,
   Mayfair, W.1.

ROYALTIES

It is illegal to produce copies of Ordnance Survey maps without the sanction of Her Majesty's Stationery Office.

Permission to reproduce maps for the purpose of Orienteering may be obtained from the Director General, Ordnance Survey, Chessington, Surrey. Application is made on an appropriate form.

The first condition of obtaining permission to copy a map is to be able to prove that the original OS map is unsuitable. In the case of Orienteering this is entirely true, for the map has to be corrected, altered and have additional material added to it to indicate private land, out-of-bounds areas, etc., before it is suitable for competition. This situation has already been accepted by the Publication Department of the OS.

The second condition is that the map reproductions are not being sold and are being used only for business or official purposes. Orienteering races under the auspices of the various regional associations are acceptable to the OS office.

Permission to reproduce an area of Ordnance Survey map may be sought for one particular reason. In this case details of the map area and number of copies, use, etc., is sent off to the OS at least a month before the event. The Survey then grant permission and indicate the royalty payable.

More convenient for the regular organiser of Orienteering competitions is a 'quarterly licence'. The holder of this licence may make as many copies of maps as he wishes for Orienteering purposes and settles his account with the OS in retrospect at quarterly intervals.

A regional officer of an Orienteering association would find this by far the most convenient way of ensuring that all reproductions printed in his area were legal. It would only be necessary for him to take stock at the end of every quarter and calculate the total sum of royalties due from his area for each of the races in which his association was involved.

The actual cost of royalties is very reasonable and is assessed on the area of the map copied and the number of copies made. For instance, 100 copies of an area of 50 square inches, about the size of most Orienteering maps, would incur a royalty of 17s. 6d.

Each reproduction must bear the acknowledgement, 'Reproduced from the Ordnance Survey map with the sanction of the Controller of H.M. Stationery Office. Crown Copyright reserved'.

The Publication Division of the OS are most helpful and co-operative. They will send all the regulations governing reproduction to anyone who applies for a licence to reproduce Ordnance Survey maps.

112

The British Orienteering Federation

FORMATION

The inaugural meeting of the B.O.F. was held at Barnard Castle on 17th June, 1967, under the chairmanship of Mr. A. L. Colbeck, M.B.E., Regional Officer of the Central Council of Physical Recreation (North East). The object of forming a British Orienteering Federation as the single national controlling body in the United Kingdom was really a natural form of development of the sport. In the first instance it was not possible for either the English or Scottish Associations to become members of the International Orienteering Federation, because the rules of the I.O.F. state that only one member Association may be admitted from one country. In addition the Sports Council had expressed its wish for the formation of a single National Controlling Body. The Officers of the English and Scottish Association had met in March, 1967, and agreed on a draft constitution for the new Federation. Whilst the English Orienteering Association has now disbanded, it must be stressed that the Scottish Association still exists as the constituent association governing Orienteering in Scotland. The Executive Committee of the new Federation is made up of two representatives from each of the existing constituent associations in England and two from Scotland. Constitution provides for similar representation of two representatives from Wales and two from Northern Ireland when these areas have been developed.

B.O.F. NATIONAL OFFICE

The National Office was set up in business on 1st September, 1967. It is most ably run by Mrs. Patricia Norris (for her address, see Appendix I). The National Office has a number of functions:

1. As from January 1st, 1968, all entries for fixtures on the

National List should be sent to the National Office. A new and standardised entry form has been prepared.

2. The National Office offers a service to all Regional Secretaries for the typing of official letters and the duplicating of information about events, start lists, etc.

3. The National Office keeps a Master List of all members of the British Orienteering Federation. It is from this list that all News Letters, Fixture Lists and other information is sent out.

APPENDIX VI

The National Badge Scheme

A four stage badge scheme is now available for orienteerers. Badges will be awarded for personal success in THREE Orienteering races. The distinctive metal lapel badge depicts a red and white Orienteering marker surrounded by sprigs of evergreen leaves. It will certainly elicit comment and arouse interest wherever it is seen.

THE IRON BADGE. This will be awarded to all classes of orienteerers, e.g. boys and girls under 15, juniors (under 18), intermediates (under 21) and seniors. *Qualification:* To finish in three Orienteering races (day or night cross-country events only) that are on either the Regional or National Fixture Lists.

THE BRONZE BADGE. Available for Junior, Intermediates and Seniors. *Qualification:* To finish in three races on the National Fixture List in times that are better than the average of the first three finishers plus 100 per cent of this time. For example:

1st Edwards	52 min. 26 sec.
2nd Blake	58 min. 13 sec.
3rd Harris	64 min. 09 sec.

Average of first three=58 min. 16 sec.

Pass time for Bronze badge would be 116 min. 32 sec.

THE SILVER BADGE. Available for Juniors, Intermediates and Seniors. *Qualification:* To finish in three races on the National Fixture List in times that are better than the average of the first three finishers plus 50 per cent of this time. In the above example all times better than 87 min. 24 sec. (58.16+29.08) would be valid.

THE GOLD BADGE. Available for Seniors only. *Qualification:* To finish in 3 races on the National Fixture List in times that are better than the average of the first three finishers plus 25 per cent of this time. In the above example all times better than 72 min. 50 sec. (58.16+14.34) would be valid.

Note 1. Successes gained in one age class will still count toward a badge even if the orienteerer moves on into an upper age group while competing for his award.

Note 2. Orienteerers competing out of their age class will receive no special consideration.

Note 3. Only point (cross-country) type Orienteering races will be considered (Score, Line and other types of competition will not be eligible for consideration).

How to apply for your badge. When you have achieved THREE valid results in events held after October 2nd, 1967 which will qualify you for a particular badge, please send the details to the National Statistician, Mr. Tony Walker, 65 Kingsmead Avenue, Worcester Park, Surrey, together with 2/- (payable to the British Orienteering Federation). Your results will be verified and if acceptable your Badge posted to you within three days.

INDEX

Page numbers in *italic* type refer to illustrations